FASHION FUN

FASHION FUN

MELINDA COSS

CRESCENT BOOKS
NEW YORK • AVENEL

Dedication:
For Suzanne -
get some glitter and get a life

First published in 1995 by Collins & Brown Ltd, London
This 1995 edition published by Crescent Books, distributed by Random House Value Publishing, Inc.
40 Engelhard Avenue, Avenel, New Jersey 07001.

Random House
New York • Toronto • London • Sydney • Auckland

Copyright © Collins & Brown Ltd 1995

Edited by Emma Callery
Designed by Carole Perks
Photography by Jon Stewart
Styling by Barbara Stewart
Illustrations by Steve Dew and Delia Elliman

A CIP catalog reecord for this book is available from the Library of Congress.

ISBN 0-517-14134-5

10 9 8 7 6 5 4 3 2 1

Typeset by Art Photoset Ltd.
Color reproduction by Pixel Tech, Singapore
Printed and bound in Singapore by CS Graphics

Contents

Introduction

Ask any leading fashion designer for the source of their inspiration and they will reply, 'The street'. Far from taking their styles from the colourful floating forms that appear on the catwalk, the designers have gone out there among us, seen how we choose to drape and coordinate our fashions and taken our ideas back to their studios to put the pieces together into 'A Collection'.

People relate to fashions in different ways. The young and the bold use their clothes (and hair), to make a personal statement while those with less confidence opt for colours and shapes that they feel confident in.

This book is about making personal statements, recycling and making use of some wonderful new products that allow us to personalize our clothes in interesting and practical ways. In our wardrobes (or our friends' wardrobes) we all have fashion buys that either 'seemed a good idea at the time', or that we are simply bored with. Most of us also share the problem that designer clothes are usually out of the reach of our pockets. So use this book to help you convert your boring old clothes into personal masterpieces with the minimum of expense and skill.

What it is not, is a book about the fine art of textile design: this I leave to the experts. The projects here have been produced in a matter of hours from a collection of cast-offs and the odd length of calico or plain, heavyweight muslin. Your rag bag will contain different items, and it is therefore my intention that you simply use the ideas and techniques illustrated here as a basis for your own fashion statements. You are not supposed to religiously reproduce the garments on these pages.

The second purpose of this book is to turn you into the fashion

designers of the future. The huge ranges of paints, fabrics and glitters on the market today require the minimum amount of skill to apply. On attempting one project, you may well find ideas in your head that you never knew were there. Silk painting, for example, uses many techniques, and once you have bought a set of silk paints for one project you can go on and experiment with more ambitious ideas.

Fashion, of the non-Dior type, is also about humour and I hope that you find some of the ideas behind these projects amusing. Sadly, we won't all fit into skintight body suits, but if we can't knock them out with our sleek forms we can at least stun them with our originality.

Melinda Coss.

Drying paints

Most of the decorative products used in this book take about four hours to dry. If you have the time, it is best to leave them overnight to dry really thoroughly.

Washing and ironing decorated clothes

It is probably best to wait 72 hours after applying fabric paints, glitter paints, puff paints, indeed almost all of the products used in this book, before washing your garment. To be on the safe side, never wash them above 40°F, and never, *never* tumble dry them. To iron the garments, always press on the reverse side. If you don't, you will run the risk of smudging your designs, and — even worse — getting irritating smeary blotches on your iron.

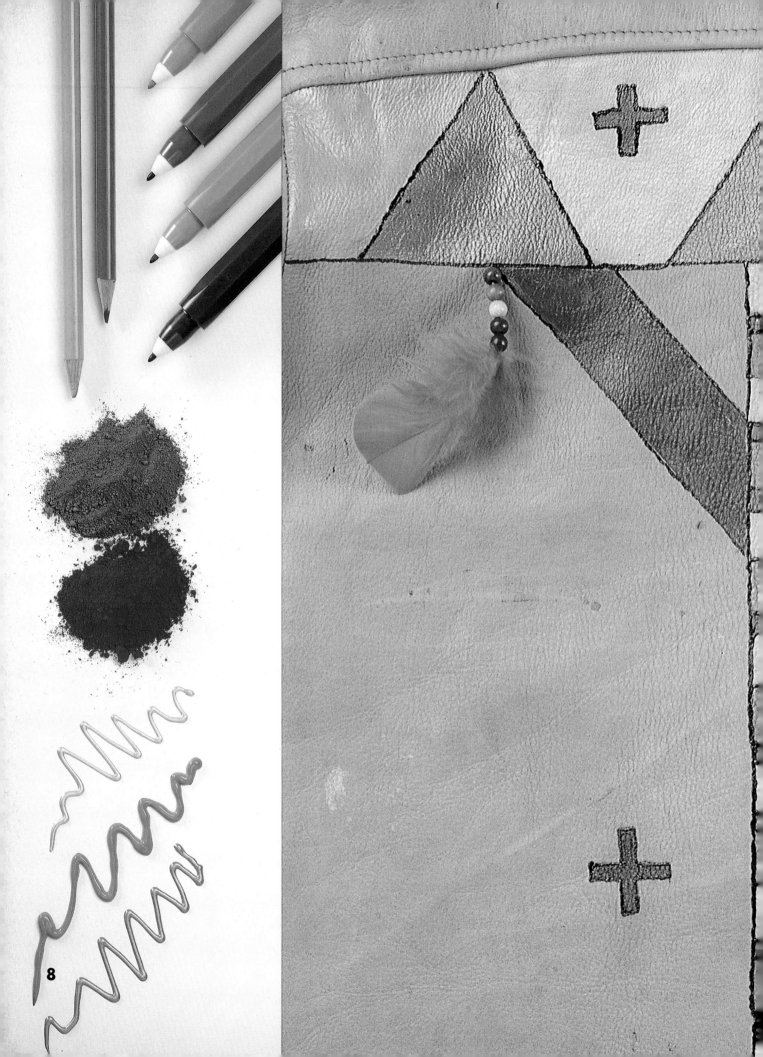

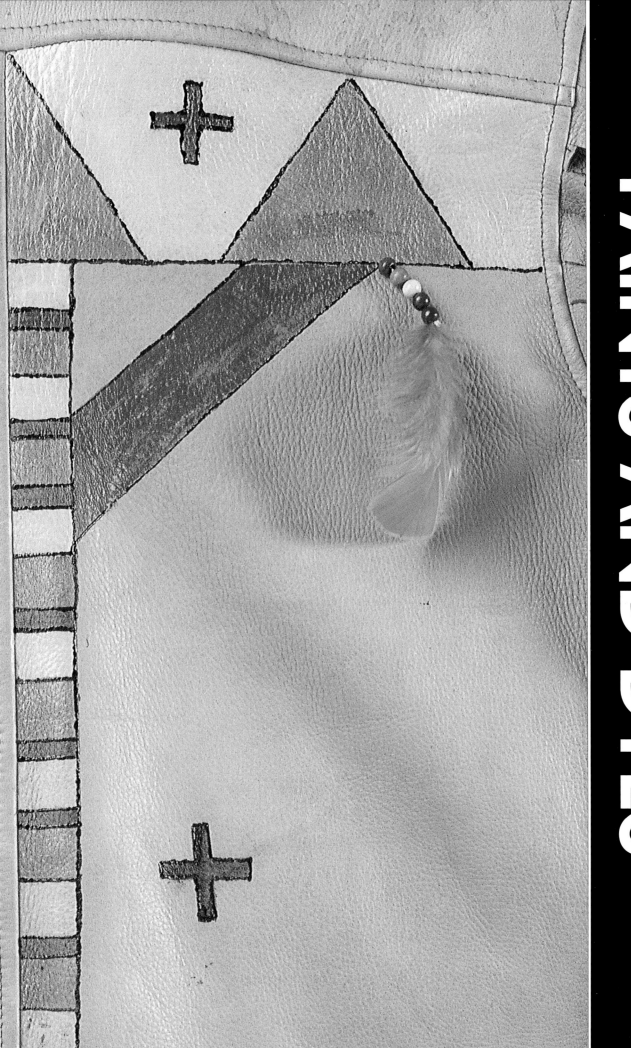

TECHNIQUES

The simplest way to decorate your clothes is to paint them, and there are numerous products on the market that will ensure your finished outfit is wearable, washable and durable. In the back of this book I provide you with stockists for the various paints I have used, but more and more exotic products are becoming available each day as manufacturers catch onto the fact that people want to decorate or make clothes that show off their own individuality. When selecting paints (and fabric pens also fall into this category), the most important thing to ascertain is that the fabric they are intended for matches the fabric you will be working on. To fix a fabric paint, check the manufacturer's instructions, but most of them can be fixed by simply ironing the back of the garment for about three minutes at a temperature that suits the fabric. You will then be able to wash them in the washing machine at a temperature of up to 60°F.

Transfer paints

Paint these onto non-absorbent paper, leave to dry and then iron onto your fabric, setting the iron between the wool and cotton temperatures. This method of working has the advantage of allowing you to make mistakes on the paper rather than on your garment. You can also produce some interesting random effects by spraying the paint onto the paper or painting around leaves or ferns. Remember that the image will be reversed when you apply it to the surface.

Sun-fading and Bleaching

During my research into tie-dying (see overleaf), I also discovered these interesting techniques where the final effects are achieved by taking colour out of fabrics rather than putting it onto them (see pages 18–19).

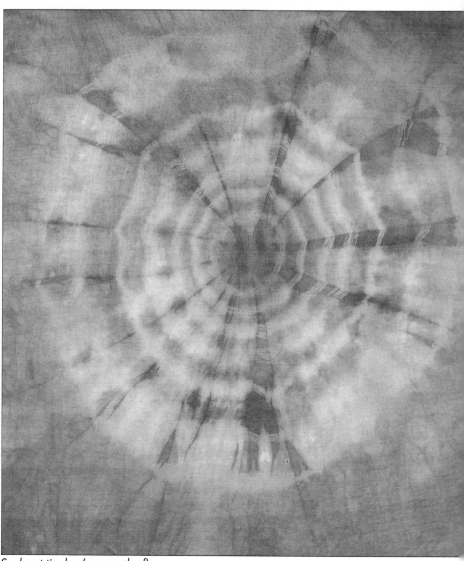

Sunburst tie-dye (see overleaf).

Photo-transfer

There is now a wonderful product on the market (see stockists) which means that you can now transfer photographs onto tee-shirts at home. It lifts the image from a colour or black and white photocopy directly onto your fabric. See Photo-transfer Tee-shirt on page 20 for a more detailed description of how this works.

Planning your design

Don't worry about your ability to draw/paint/design. Images can be traced from magazines, this book, children's colouring books, postcards and no end of other inspirational material. If a garment is for your own use or for use by your children no one will seriously object to you 'interpreting' a clever artist's image. If you don't want to make a whole picture, you could use simple basic shapes such as circles or triangles and arrange them onto a tee-shirt or jacket to make an overall pattern. You can use stencils to add lettering and create slogans and names *ad infinitum*.

Even if you feel you have no talent for design, you will be surprised at some of the images you can create using scraps of coloured paper or old photographs. One way to experiment is to cut out random shapes and arrange them on a sheet of white paper.

Another interesting experiment is to cut out a circle or an oblong of approximately 4 x 3in (10 x 7.5cm) from a sheet of paper leaving a frame behind. Lay the piece of paper over a section of a coloured photograph (from a magazine) or over a collection of randomly placed cut-outs. This can provide you with an interesting arrangement of colours and textures which you can then use as a basis for a tee-shirt design. The art of design centres around perspective and it is quite enlightening to view familiar items from unfamiliar angles.

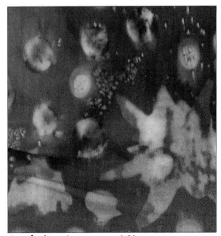

Sun-fading (see page 18).

A photo-transfer (see page 20).

Materials

There are a number of basic materials that you should arm yourself with before beginning a painting project. First, you should protect your clothing from splatters by wearing an old smock or shirt and second you should protect your work surface. I work on a kitchen table covered with a length of PVC but you could cut open a large garbage bag and use that to do the job.

You will need paintbrushes in various thicknesses according to the designs you wish to create, several jars full of clean water, some rags, a couple of saucers or jar lids to use as palettes and some thumb tacks.

Preparing fabrics

When working on tee-shirts and jumpers I found it useful to insert a sheet of cardboard between the front and the back. This has the dual purpose of protecting the back of the garment from paint and creating a taut surface for you to work on.

Single thicknesses of fabric should be stretched either by pinning them to your table with thumb tacks or by pinning them to a frame. You can purchase frames specifically designed for silk painting which can be adjusted according to the size of your fabric (see stockist information on page 94). Alternatively, you can make a simple frame by nailing together four pieces of wood (I used 2 x ½in [5 x 1cm] timber) to form a square to pin your fabric to.

All the paints I use are water-soluble. However, check the manufacturer's instructions to determine whether any special cleaning or diluting agents are necessary.

Transferring images

— for those who feel they cannot draw (but probably can). It is a simple process to transfer an image from either the templates in the back of this book or another source, such as a book illustration or poster. There are various traditional methods for doing this which I explain below, but with the availability of photocopiers the world is your oyster.

Transfer pencils These pencils can be bought from needlework, notions and general department stores. Before beginning, test the pencil on an inside hem of the garment to make sure the image will take.

Using tracing paper, or household greaseproof or parchment paper, and an ordinary pencil, trace the outline of the design of your choice. Turn the paper over and draw over the pencil lines with the transfer pencil. Place the image, transfer side down, on top of your work and press with an iron set according to the heat required for the fabric you are working on. While pressing take care not to slide the iron around as your image may slip or blur.

Cut-outs When working a simple outline I always use a cut-out. To make a cut-out you will need a soft lead pencil, some tracing paper and a thin sheet of cardboard. Trace the outline of your image with the pencil. On the back of the tracing paper, re-draw the shape over the pencil lines. Place this face down on the cardboard and scribble over the top to transfer the pencil marks. Cut around the shape with a sharp pair of scissors. You can then arrange the cut-outs on the item you wish to decorate and draw around them with a fabric pencil or pen.

Photocopies You can obtain a simple reversed image from a photocopy using the following method (note that this method will not work on synthetic fibres). Make your photocopy, enlarging or reducing it as required. Using a sponge or paintbrush, dampen the outline of the photocopied image plus the fabric with a solvent made up from one cup of white spirit or turpentine, one cup of water and a few drops of washing-up liquid. Place the dampened image face down on the fabric and lay a piece of old fabric or newspaper over the top. Iron with a very hot iron, taking care not to slide the iron around in case the image moves.

TECHNIQUE FOCUS:
Tie-dying

By tying your clothes into knots and dying them you can create some extraordinary patterns. Hot and cold water dyes are available in a vast range of colours that will transform white clothes, whether they are shirts, tee-shirts or underwear. After seeing the results, I felt tempted to tie-dye sheets and use them instead of wallpaper to line my studio walls. The effects you can achieve are brilliant and once you have dyed your first garment, beware! All kinds of inspirational ideas are bound to surface.

Wonderful swirly patterns can be achieved with the tie-dye technique. What you are actually doing is folding and binding your fabrics in various ways so that when they are dipped in the dye some areas will remain untouched. There are a number of tried and tested ways of folding your fabric that will produce standard results. Whichever effect — or combination of effects you choose — follow the steps opposite for the best results.

Materials
Dye
Coldfix
Salt
Plastic bucket
Rubber gloves
Prewashed and dampened garment
Rubber bands
Paintbrush (*medium*)
Plastic bag
Detergent

1 Place the dye, coldfix and salt in a bucket and mix it to a paste with a small amount of water (wear rubber gloves to avoid staining your hands with the dye). Add the remaining water, mixing thoroughly.

2 Tie the garment in your chosen way (*see opposite*).

3 Paint the dye onto the garment with a paintbrush, pushing the colour into the folds.

4 Place the garment in a plastic bag, seal and leave overnight.

5 Remove from the bag, take off the rubber bands and rinse the garment in cold water until the water runs clear.

6 Wash in hot water with a normal laundry detergent. Dry away from direct heat and sunlight.

The step-by-step pictures opposite show you three ways of tying material. Experiment with combinations and other ways of folding the fabric — perhaps you could tie some knots, or bind the garment with one long piece of string.

These leggings and grandad shirt have been marble tie-dyed. The fabric was painted first with yellow, then red dye.

Sunburst Tie-dye

1 Dampen the tee-shirt and lay it out flat with the back facing you. Place a stone in the centre.

2 Bind the stone in place with a rubber band. Twisting the cloth as you go, bind the remaining fabric at intervals with rubber bands to form concentric circles.

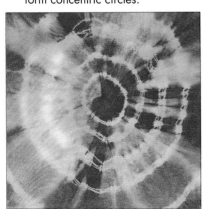

3 The finished sunburst tie-dye. Notice how the elastic bands have formed the concentric rings.

Rectangular Tie-dye

1 Dampen the tee-shirt and fold it in pleats.

2 Bind it at regular intervals with elastic bands.

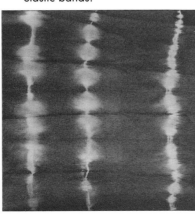

3 The finished rectangular tie-dye. the pleated folds have picked up more dye than the rest of the fabric giving this fabric still more variation in colour.

Marble Tie-dye

1 Dampen the tee-shirt and then scrunch it into a ball. Tightly bind it with elastic bands, criss-crossing the surface as you put them on.

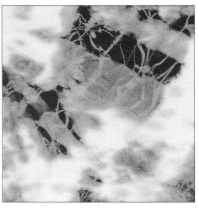

2 The finished marbled tie-dye. Because the fabric was scrunched up the variation in tone is quite dramatic.

Blue Sunburst Tee-shirt and Marbled Shorts

If you are tie-dying two garments to be worn together, don't feel restricted to dying them in the same style — mix and match the effects. Go crazy!

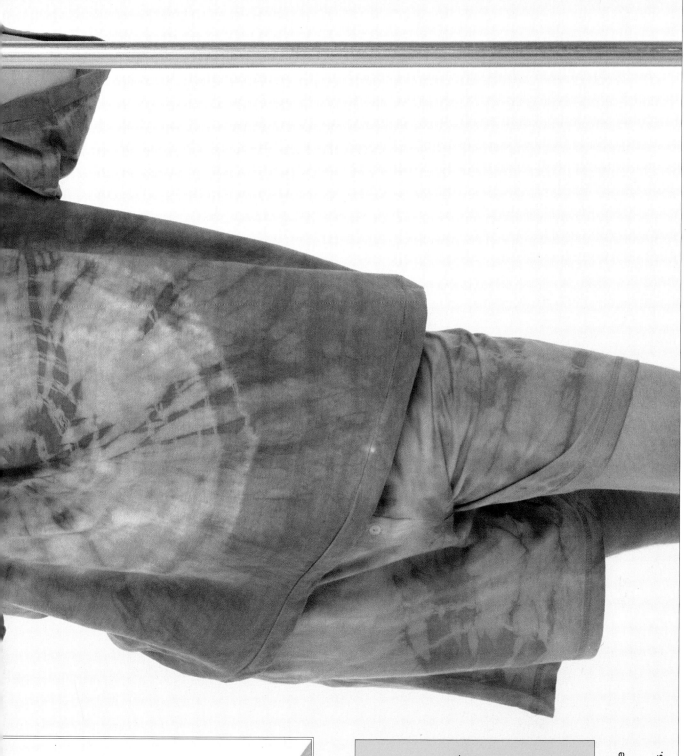

Materials

Prewashed, damp, white cotton tee-
shirt and shorts
1 tin cold water dye (*french navy*)
1 sachet coldfix
16 fl oz (500ml/½ cup) warm water
2oz (60g/¼ cup) salt
Plastic bucket
Rubber gloves
Old wooden spoon
Stone
Rubber bands
Paintbrush (2 ½in [6cm] wide)
Plastic bag

For detailed instructions on tie-dying the
garments to achieve sunburst and
marbled effects, see the Tie-dying
Technique Focus on the previous pages.

Striped Tee-shirt

You can, of course, experiment by using fabric paints as an alternative to dyes to create a tie-dyed effect. If you use silk paints your garment will come out several shades lighter than the colour in the bottle.

Materials
Tee-shirt
Fabric paint (*emerald green*)
Rubber bands
Paintbrush (2½in [6cm] wide)
Plastic bag

1 Pleat and bind the tee-shirt as described in the Rectangular tie-dying method on page 13.

2 Dilute the fabric paint one part paint with two parts water and then apply it to the wet tee-shirt with a paintbrush.

3 Leave the painted garment in a sealed plastic bag over night, hang it out to dry and iron on the back to fix the colour.

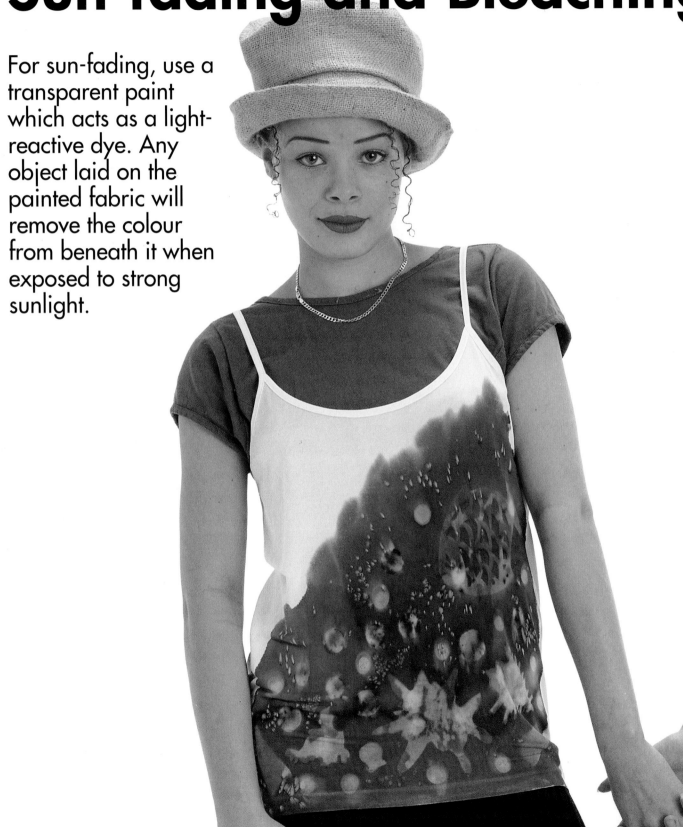

Sun-fading and Bleaching

For sun-fading, use a transparent paint which acts as a light-reactive dye. Any object laid on the painted fabric will remove the colour from beneath it when exposed to strong sunlight.

For the Sun-faded Tee-shirt
Materials
White or light coloured tee-shirt
Transparent paint
Paintbrush (*broad*)
Paper cut-outs or objects (*eg shells, leaves, feathers*)

1 Dampen your garment.

2 Dilute the paint, mixing one part paint with two parts water.

3 Paint a wash quickly onto the garment to form a background.

4 Lay the paper cut-outs or objects on the painted background and leave in sunlight, without disturbing, until the fabric is completely dry.

5 Remove the objects and press the garment on the wrong side, setting the iron's temperature to suit the fabric.

Note: Avoid windy days...the cut-outs or objects will blow away.

For the Bleached Tee-shirt
Materials
Rubber gloves
Household bleach
Sleeveless tee-shirt
Dye (*optional*)
Paintbrush
Detergent

1 Wearing rubber gloves and working on a protected surface, mix one part water with one part bleach.

2 Splatter the bleach mixture over a pre-dyed garment or one that you have dyed yourself.

3 If you feel ambitious, paint the bleach on with a paintbrush to create your own negative designs.

4 Once the design is complete, wash the garment.

Extraordinary effects can be achieved by sun-fading (the tee-shirt on the left) and bleaching (right). Experiment with all sorts of painting techniques and colours.

19

Photo-transfer Tee-shirt

You can wear your favourite photograph with the help of some transfer fluid. If you are printing onto a coloured tee-shirt, make sure you only paint the exact area of the photostat with white fabric paint before beginning.

Materials
Tee-shirt (*white*)
Piece of plastic
Fabric paint (*white*) (*optional*)
Iron and ironing board
Photocopy of your favourite photograph (*enlarged to the required size*)
Waxed paper or foil
Transfer fluid
Paintbrush (*broad*)
Kitchen paper towels
Rolling pin
Sponge

1 Wash, dry and press your tee-shirt. Insert the piece of plastic between the front and back.

2 If the tee-shirt is coloured, paint the area you are printing on with white fabric paint (on dark colours you will need two or three coats of paint). Heat fix the paint between coats and after the final one by pressing on the wrong side of the fabric with the iron set to cotton.

3 Place your photocopy, right side up, on a sheet of waxed paper or foil. Brush over it generously with the transfer fluid until you cannot see the picture beneath. Carefully pick up the wet print and lay it pasted side down on the tee-shirt. Press it down to make sure there are no wrinkles.

4 Place a kitchen paper towel over the print and, using the rolling pin, lightly press the paper to the fabric rolling it in alternate directions. Do this for one minute and check that the edges have stuck down. Remove the paper and use it to blot any excess paste. Leave it to dry, preferably overnight or for a minimum of four hours.

5 Place a water-soaked sponge on the image and let it soak in for a few minutes until the paper is thoroughly wet. With your finger or sponge gently rub over the image until the paper can be rolled off. The top layer of paper will remove easily and should be pulled to the centre of the image and picked up in a paper towel. Use the sponge to rub off the initial layer of fuzzy paper.

6 Leave to dry, then remove any fuzzy residue with a moist sponge. Leave to dry again and then seal the image by wiping a few drops of the transfer fluid into the grain of your transfer, making sure it is completely covered. Leave to dry.

Washing: Do not wash for the first 72 hours and then wash either by hand in cool water or in a washing machine on a wool wash. Do not dry clean and do not iron directly onto the design.

Stencilled

ee-shirts

Brighten up a plain white tee-shirt with a simple rose stencil, or use an alphabet stencil which you can make yourself or buy in a stationer's.

TECHNIQUE FOCUS:
Making a Stencil

Materials
Acetate
Felt-tip pen
Craft knife
Cutting board

1 Lay a piece of acetate over the outline and then carefully trace over the design with a felt-tip pen.

2 Carefully cut out the petal shapes and the leaf shapes with a craft knife over the cutting board.

For the Alphabet Tee-shirt
Materials
Tee-shirt (*white*)
Alphabet stencil
Fabric paints (*various colours*)
Fabric markers (*various colours*)

1 Stencil the letters onto the tee-shirt using the paints and markers. Leave to dry.

2 Outline the letters in freehand with the black fabric marker.

3 Leave to dry and then iron on the wrong side for three minutes with the iron set to cotton. Your finished tee-shirt will then be machine-washable at a temperature of up to 60°F.

For the Rose Tee-shirt
Materials
A4 (*8½ x 11½in*) sheet of clear acetate
Felt-tip pen
Craft knife
Cutting board
Fabric paints (*red, yellow, green*)
Saucer
Tee-shirt (*white*)
Dressmaker's pins
Masking tape
Stencil brush
Iron and ironing board

1 Enlarge the rose design on page 88 on a photocopier to an appropriate size and then make the stencil as shown in the Technique Focus to the left.

2 Mix your paints on a saucer so that you have various shades of red and orange, and two shades of green.

3 With the dressmaker's pins, mark positions for ten roses: eight on the front and one on each sleeve. Attach your stencil in position with masking tape and paint the flower petals with the various shades of colour, starting at the centre of each area and working out.

4 When the flowers have dried, add leaves, stencilling them in shades of green.

5 Leave to dry and then iron on the wrong side for three minutes with the iron set to cotton. Your finished tee-shirt will then be machine-washable at a temperature of up to 60°F.

23

Christopher the Crab

This fun kid's tee-shirt has been painted directly onto the fabric.

Materials
Prewashed tee-shirt
Tracing paper
Pencil
Cardboard
Scissors
Fabric marker pen (*black*)
Fabric paints (*lemon, vermilion, orange, pink, green*)
Sponge or flat-headed stencil brush
2 x ½in (*12mm*) googly eyes
Fabric glue

1 Enlarge the template on page 90 on a photocopier to an appropriate size. Then trace it and cut it out (see Transferring Images on page 11).

2 Insert a piece of cardboard between the front and the back of the tee-shirt to stop the paint going through to the back.

3 Arrange your cut-outs on the front of the tee-shirt.

4 Draw around them with the black fabric marker pen.

5 Remove the cut-outs and draw in the mouth. Dab in the colours randomly using either the sponge or stencil brush. The colours on most fabric paints are intermixable so you should be able to achieve all sorts of wild and wonderful combinations.

6 If required, add some swirls to represent seaweed and a few criss-cross lines around the crab and on the sleeves.

7 Glue on the googly eyes.

8 Leave the paint and glue to dry and then iron on the wrong side for three minutes with the iron set to cotton. Your finished tee-shirt will then be machine-washable at a temperature of up to 60°F.

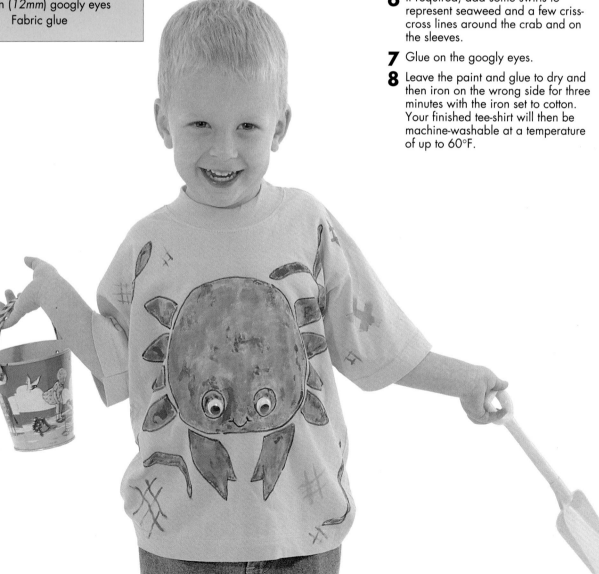

Patricia Parrot Leggings

With a cheerful and colourful parrot like this around, what more would you need to brighten up your day?

Materials
Prewashed leggings
Cardboard
Greaseproof or parchment paper, or tracing paper
Transfer pencil
Iron and ironing board
Fabric paints (*green, red, yellow, white*)
Paintbrush (*medium*)
2 x ½in (*12mm*) googly eyes
Fabric glue

---

1 Insert a piece of cardboard down one leg of the leggings to stop the paint seeping through onto the back of the leggings.

2 Trace the template on page 89 onto the greaseproof or parchment paper, or tracing paper, and use the transfer pencil and iron to position it on the leggings (see Transferring Images on page 11).

3 Paint in the feathers mixing white with green to form various shades of green.

4 Paint in the face and body in reds and yellows.

5 Glue on the googly eyes.

6 Leave the paint and glue to dry and then iron on the wrong side for three minutes with the iron set to cotton. Your finished tee-shirt will then be machine-washable at a temperature of up to 60°F.

Note: The white paint has been mixed with the green, red and yellow to give lighter tones for shading and for the outline of the design.

25

Sun and Star Tee-shirts

As a general rule, the best effects are achieved when working on a light-coloured fabric. However, subtle and surprising results can come from applying fabric paints on darker coloured fabrics.

For the Astral Star Tee-shirt
Materials
Prewashed tee-shirt
Greaseproof or parchment paper, or tracing paper
Transfer pencil
Iron and ironing board
Felt-tip marker pens (*black, magenta, yellow, light green, blue*)

1 Using a photocopier, enlarge the template on page 87 to an appropriate size. Trace the outline onto the greaseproof or parchment paper, or tracing paper, and use the transfer pencil and iron to position it on the tee-shirt (see Transferring Images on page 11).

2 Draw over the transferred lines with the black felt-tip marker, and then fill in the colours according to the template.

3 Leave to dry and then iron on the wrong side for three minutes with the iron set to cotton. Your finished tee-shirt will then be machine-washable at a temperature of up to 60°F.

Note: You can get subtle shaded effects by drawing one colour over another. The possibilities are endless. These pens would also be great used with Celtic designs. Get a book on them from your library and experiment.

For the Happy Sun Tee-shirt
Materials
Prewashed tee-shirt (*purple*)
Greaseproof or parchment paper, or tracing paper
Transfer pencil
Iron and ironing board
Fabric liner (*black*)
Paintbrushes (*broad, fine*)
Fabric paints (*yellow, red, opaque white, black*)
Glitter liner (*gold*)

1 Using a photocopier, enlarge the template on page 86 to an appropriate size. Trace the outline onto the greaseproof or parchment paper, or tracing paper, and use the transfer pencil and iron to position it on the tee-shirt (see Transferring Images on page 11).

2 Use the black fabric liner to outline the main body of the design and the circles in each sun point. Leave to dry for at least an hour.

3 Using the broad paintbrush, fill in the centre of the sun with the yellow fabric paint and the points in red, mixed with a little white.

4 Leave to dry then paint in the nose, eyes and outline of the mouth in black using the fine brush.

5 Add the glitter details with the gold glitter liner. Either squeeze directly from the bottle for the finer lines, or apply it with a paintbrush for the thicker lines. Leave to dry. Add the black magic liner details, ie the triangles and blobs in the centre of the circles.

6 Paint in the mouth and cheeks in red and the eyeballs in white. Add glitter to the cheeks by first applying it with the fine brush and then adding a swirl straight from the tube.

7 Leave to dry and then iron on the wrong side for three minutes with the iron set to cotton. Your finished tee-shirt will then be machine-washable at a temperature of up to 60°F.

27

Watercolour
Tunic

This silk tunic was originally cream but it was stained. However, with the help of silk paints and a watercolour painting technique, I've turned a vice into a virtue.

Materials
Silk tunic (cream)
Towel
Silk paints (lavender, yellow, pink)
Saucer
Water
Soft paintbrush (broad) or a sponge
Iron and ironing board

1 Open up the tunic and lay it on a table, over a towel, right side up. Dampen thoroughly.

2 Dilute and mix one of the silk paints in a saucer with the paintbrush or sponge. Wash the colour over the fabric, painting with broad strokes or applying with the sponge. Add subsequent colours in the same way, letting the shades run into each other until the garment is completely covered.

3 Iron on the wrong side over a towel at a medium temperature to fix.

Painted Leather Jerkin

I bought this jerkin in a street market for a very reasonable price. The reason it was so cheap was because the sleeves were half the size they should have been so I decided to make a feature of them.

3 Paint each area with the fabric paints and then outline them with the fabric liner. Some fabric paints also act as a glue, so you could add beads or mirrors directly to the paint as you go.

4 To finish, thread lengths of cotton cord through the jerkin and then through five wooden beads. Tie a feather to the end and bring the threads back through the beads and the jerkin, securing them on the inside.

1 Rip out the lining, cut off the cuffs and cut the sleeves into ½in (12mm) strips. The fringe at the bottom of this jerkin already existed but if you don't like the length of your jerkin, you can fringe the bottom yourself.

2 To give the jerkin a Native American feel about it, first draw simple geometric shapes, such as triangles and stripes, on the jerkin with chalk, using a ruler as a guide. Then, when you are happy with the results, go over the lines with a ballpoint pen.

Materials
Leather jerkin
Scissors
Chalk
Ruler
Ballpoint pen
Fabric paints (aqua, bronze, pink)
Fabric liner (black)
Small mirrors (optional)
Beads (optional)
Cotton cord
Wooden beads
Feathers

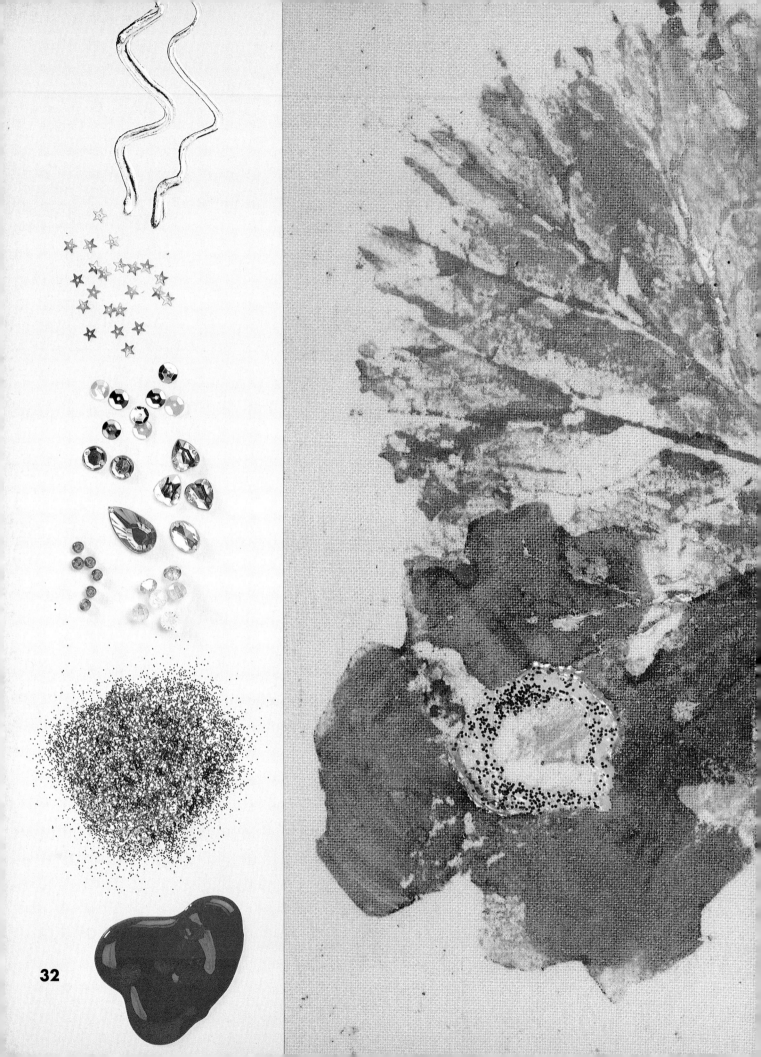

TECHNIQUES

Glittering

Glitters that can be sealed to your garment with diluted glue are available in a large range of colours. To the creatively minded, this opens the door to no end of weird and wonderful design ideas. My only warning is that the glitter flies and settles in every conceivable nook and cranny so it is best to work outside on a windless day.

You can put garments decorated with glitter in the washing machine. Some of it may come off so wash them in a bag (a pillow case, for example) to avoid getting glitter onto your other clothes. If you want to top up the glitter again afterwards, this is quite easy — simply spray on some more.

Multi-coloured glitter (see page 39).

Printing

For those who cannot draw, wonderful patterns can be achieved using a printing technique and fabric paint. You can print with virtually anything from a rubber stamp to a piece of string but for the purposes of this book I have utilised that nourishing piece of matter known as the potato (see Floral Potato-print Sarong, page 42). Potatoes can be cut into a vast number of shapes and you can make your designs extremely intricate. However, I have always found that simple shapes used with unusual colours give the best results. Once your potato has been cut you can store it in the refrigerator in a plastic bag for up to three days.

In the printing section, I have also used fresh leaves dipped in paint and then pressed against fabric. Several projects have been made from lengths of calico or heavyweight muslin, hemmed top and bottom, and then gathered on elastic or tied to form skirts and tops. You do not need to be a dressmaker to make your own clothes. Experiment by tying fabrics around you in different ways for fun summer beachwear.

Potato print (see page 45).

Leaf print (see page 43).

Silk painting

Silk painting can become obsessive because the simple techniques produce stunning results. With the projects in this section I hope I can inspire you to use silk paints to their full advantage (see also the Watercolour Tunic on pages 28–9). Here I have experimented with the marvellously bright effects achieved by using water-based gutta on plain ties that can be bought ready to paint. A sprinkling of salt on wet silk paint draws out the colour, creating a speckled effect, as shown on pages 46–7. I have also decorated a simple silk waistcoat with a plain fleur de lis motif. By drawing the outlines as a regular pattern I have created an all-over design.

Gutta paint (see page 49).

TECHNIQUE FOCUS:
Foiling

One of the greatest new innovations in clothes art has to be transfer foil. This works on the principle of traditional gold leaf. You buy the foil in sheets, which are available in a vast selection of colours and special effects, including hologram, rainbow and swirl. You apply the foil cold, over a special glue, or over a special iron-on transfer. Your finished piece is then hand-washable. While I only glued foil on garments, when using the glue rather than transfer method, these products can be applied to virtually any surface from fabric to wood.

Materials
Prewashed garment
Transfer glue
Transfer foil

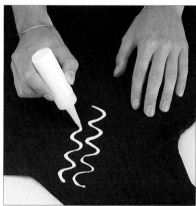

1 Squeeze the glue directly onto the garment. You might prefer to draw your design using tailor's chalk first, or else draw it freehand with the glue. Leave the glue to dry. It is preferable to leave it overnight, but you could use a hairdryer to speed things up. The glue is ready once it becomes clear rather than the opaque white appearance it has when it is first squeezed out of the bottle. It should also feel slightly tacky.

2 Take a sheet of gold foil and lay it, coloured side up, over the glue. Press gently over the raised shape with your forefinger.

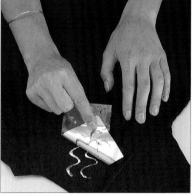

3 Slowly peel back the foil to reveal the pattern beneath. If any glue gaps show, repeat the process. Repeat until the whole design is covered in foil.

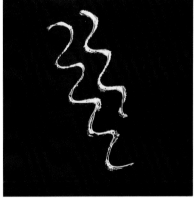

4 The finished foiled pattern. Don't feel that you have to restrict yourself to using single colours on each part of the design. You could, for example, use several colours on a swirl such as this, blending them into each other.

Permanent Jewelry

You will never have to worry about losing your jewelry again with these foiled and blobbed paint-effect chains.

Materials

Prewashed tee-shirt (*black*)
Transfer glue
Tailor's chalk
Transfer foils (*gold, silver, purple*)
Fabric glitter (*gold*)
Three-dimensional pearl fabric paints (*pearl, gold*)
8 large rhinestones

1 Using the transfer glue straight from the bottle squeeze out a line of ovals for your gold chain, starting at the right side of the neck and finishing at the left side. Leave ¼in (6mm) between each oval and don't worry if the chain looks crooked — it adds to the charm.

2 Repeat step 1, but make a smaller chain with smaller links directly under the neck. Leave 1in (2.5cm) spaces for the rhinestones.

3 With the tailor's chalk, draw in a simple shape for a pendant. Be creative and do your own thing but keep it simple. Go over the chalk outline with the transfer glue.

4 Leave the glue to dry (see Technique Focus on page 35).

5 To make raised links, add small links between each gold oval with the glue. Leave to dry once more.

6 Take a sheet of gold foil and press it gently over the chain repeating until the whole chain is covered in gold foil (see Technique Focus on page 35).

7 Repeat step 6 using silver foil on the shorter length of chain.

8 Pour the gold glitter over the pendant shape. Leave to dry and shake off excess glitter.

9 Add glue and purple foil decoration to the centre of the pendant, if required, using the same foiling technique.

10 To make the pearl strands, squeeze blobs on either side of the neck directly from the bottle of pearl fabric paint. The pearls should stretch down below the gold chain and pendant. Make a cluster of blobs to represent a knot and then a loop of blobs at the bottom.

11 Using the transfer glue, stick the rhinestones on the silver chain and in the centre of the pendant.

12 Join the silver links with gold three-dimensional paint blobs.

Glitter Catsuit

So easy and so effective, turn a simple black catsuit into a real dazzler with glue and many different shades of glitter.

Materials
1 black cat suit
Newspaper
Fabric glue
Water
Bottle with diffuser spray cap
Fabric glitter (blue, gold, silver, pink)
Bottle glitter paint (silver)

1 Cover the floor with newspaper and lay the catsuit on top.

2 Dilute the glue, one part water to one part glue, and pour it into a diffuser spray bottle, shaking it well.

3 Randomly sprinkle the different-coloured glitters all over the hat.

4 Hold the glue bottle approximately 6in (15cm) from the surface of the hat and spray the glue all over the glittered areas.

5 Leave for 15 minutes, then spray again. Repeat twice more and leave to dry for 15 minutes.

6 Using silver glitter paint directly from the bottle, draw star shapes randomly over the glitter.

7 Shake thoroughly - outside! (Take a handkerchief with you as you will probably sneeze.)

NB Your finished catsuit can be machine-washed on a delicate cycle. Repeated washing will result in the loss of some glitter but this can be easily re-applied.

Using the same techniques as for the Glitter Catsuit on the previous pages, brighten up your old black hat and bra.

40

Starry Night Hat and Matching Bra

Materials

For the Hat
Black hat (*straw or felt*)
Newspaper
Fabric glue
Water
Bottle with diffuser spray cap
Fabric glitter (*blue, gold, silver, pink*)
Bottle glitter paint (*silver*)

For the Bra
Cotton bra (*black*)
1yd (*1m*) of 1in (*2.5cm*)-wide lace trim (*black*)
Fabric glue
Fabric glitter (*gold, red*)
Water
Bottle with diffuser spray cap
6 rhinestones (*various sizes*)
Paintbrush

Decorating the hat

Work in the same way as the catsuit on the previous page, but spray diluted glue over the hat once before applying the glitter.

Decorating the bra

1 Cut a length of black lace long enough to fit around the bottom of the bra.

2 Using glue straight from the bottle, paint a line around the bottom edge of the bra and glue the top edge of lace onto it. Apply a strip of lace to the 'V'-line at the top of the bra in the same way.

3 Paint glue along all the stitched seams and sprinkle gold glitter over the top. Leave to dry for 15 minutes then shake off excess glitter.

4 Dilute the glue as in step 2 of the Glitter Catsuit (see page 39), spray over the lower bra cups and sprinkle on red glitter. Leave to dry.

5 Spray glue over the red glitter and apply gold glitter generously. Spray once more and leave to dry and then spray twice more, leaving 15 minutes between each application and adding extra glitter if required.

6 Arrange rhinestones at the centre of the bra and glue into position with undiluted glue.

Floral Potato-print Sarong

This length of calico has been printed with potatoes and leaves and then embellished with three-dimensional fabric paints and glitter. Tie it around you as a glamorous beach wrap.

Materials

Calico or heavyweight muslin (*long enough to wrap around you 1½ times*)
Leaves
Saucer
Fabric paints (*green, blue, yellow, white, red*)
Potato
Kitchen paper towels
Felt-tip pen
Kitchen knife or craft knife
Paintbrush
Three-dimensional fabric paint (*yellow, pink*)
Fabric glitter (*red*)
1yd (*1m*) of 1½in (*4cm*)-wide ribbon

TECHNIQUE FOCUS:
Making Potato Prints

Materials
Potato
Kitchen knife or craft knife
Felt-tip pen (*optional*)
Fabric paints
Saucer
Paintbrush

1 Cut the potato in half and wipe the cut sides with a piece of kitchen paper. Either cut the potato freehand with a sharp knife, or for a more complicated pattern draw the outline onto the potato with a felt-tip pen. Cut away the outside lines first and then remove the more detailed parts.

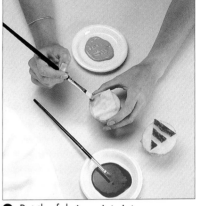

2 Put the fabric paints into a saucer and paint onto the raised parts of the potato.

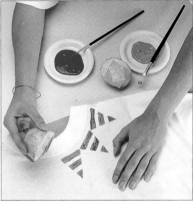

3 Print directly onto the fabric, topping up the paint as necessary. To use the potato for another colour, simply wash the potato thoroughly and repeat steps 2 and 3.

1 Wash, dry and press the fabric and hem the top and bottom to the required length.

2 Wash the leaves, and lay one on a saucer containing various shades of green fabric paint (mix the green with blue or yellow to get different shades). When the leaf is covered in paint, press it onto the fabric. Repeat randomly over the material.

3 Prepare the potato as described in the Technique Focus above. With a felt-tip pen draw a flower shape onto the cut half. My flower consists of four petals and a round centre. With the kitchen knife or craft knife cut away the areas you do not want to print, that is, the surround of the flower and the centre.

4 Mix the fabric paints to make various shades of red and purple. Paint the required colour onto the cut half of the potato and press onto the fabric, slightly overlapping a leaf. Wash the painted potato thoroughly and dry with kitchen paper. Repeat the print in a second colour, overlapping the first flower. Leave to dry.

5 With the iron set to cotton, press for three minutes on the reverse side of the flower designs.

6 Highlight the centres of the flowers with the three-dimensional fabric paints sprinkled over with glitter while the paint is still wet. Leave to dry.

7 Cut off one third of the ribbon and stitch this short piece to the top right-hand corner of the fabric. Stitch the longer piece to the top left-hand corner, wrap the fabric around your waist and tie a bow at the side.

Child's Potato-print Skirt, Top and Bag

To make the skirt, thread elastic through the top hem once the side seam has been joined together with right sides facing.

Materials
Calico or heavyweight muslin
Needle
Cotton thread
Potato
Kitchen paper towels
Felt-tip pen (*optional*)
Kitchen knife or craft knife
Saucer
Paintbrush
Fabric paints (*fluorescent pink, fluorescent orange*)
Fabric glitter (*red, pink*)
Length of 1in (*2.5cm*) wide elastic to fit comfortably around the waist (*skirt only*)
4 x ¾in (*2cm*) eyelet rings and an applicator (*bag only*)
2yd (*2m*) of string (*bag only*)
Fabric glue (*bag only*)

Fabric quantities

For the skirt: wide enough to wrap around the body 1½ times and as long as necessary plus 12in (30cm) seam allowances

For the top: wide enough to wrap around the chest, plus allow extra for tying, and 6in (15cm) deep

For the bag: two pieces each measuring 8½ x 6in (22 x 15cm)

Making and decorating the skirt

1 Wash, dry and press the calico or heavyweight muslin. Turn the top edge over twice to form a 3in (7.5cm) hem and machine-stitch seam into place. Hem the bottom to the desired length of skirt.

2 Cut the potato as described in the Technique Focus on the previous page. For this design, cut away the outside of the triangle first and then two pairs of horizontal lines to divide the triangle into three sections.

3 Paint the cut potato pink and press it onto the fabric. Repeat four times printing in a circle so that the point of the triangle forms the centre. While the paint is still wet, sprinkle a small amount of the glitters over the centre.

4 Wash your potato thoroughly and repeat step 3 using orange. Repeat until your fabric is covered with printed flowers. Print single triangles in alternate colours around the waistband and between the flower shapes. Leave to dry.

5 With the iron set to cotton, press the wrong side of the fabric for three minutes.

6 Stitch up the side seam, with right sides facing, and insert the elastic in the waistband.

Making the top

1 Hem the top and bottom of the fabric band and decorate as for the skirt.

2 To wear, either cross the band at the centre front and tie around the neck or wrap it around your chest and tie it at the back or front.

Making the bag

1 Turn over and stitch 3in (7.5cm) seams on one short end of each piece of fabric to form a border. Following the manufacturer's instructions, attach two eyelets through the double thickness of each piece of fabric. Position them 1in (2.5cm) in from each side and halfway down the 3in (7.5cm) borders.

2 Print the borders with three inverted triangles in orange, and then print randomly on the rest of the fabric, highlighting with glitter as for the skirt. Iron fix at a cotton setting, pressing for three minutes on the wrong side of the fabric.

3 Sew up the side and bottom seams, with right sides facing, and then turn the right way out. Loop the string through the eyelets tying it in a knot at the centre to form a handle.

45

Gutta Painted Ties

Here are two stunning ties whose pattern outlines have been drawn using gutta which has then been filled in with bright coloured paints. You can buy plain ties ready to paint (see stockist information).

For the Floral Tie
Materials
Tracing paper
Pencil
Lightweight cardboard
Craft knife
White silk tie
Disappearing pen
Water-based gutta (*silver*)
Silk paints (*orange, lavender, yellow, pink, purple*)
Saucers
Soft paintbrush (*medium*)
Table salt

1 Trace the template on page 88 and transfer it onto cardboard and cut it out with the craft knife (see Transferring Images on page 11).

2 Place your cut-out on the tie and draw around it with the disappearing pen. Move the template around, drawing in the outline, overlapping from flower to flower until the front of the tie is completely covered.

3 Holding the gutta just above the tie and squeezing it straight from the tube, trace over the drawn lines in silver. Check the gutta lines to make sure there are no gaps in them, and leave to dry thoroughly.

4 With the paintbrush, drop slightly diluted colours onto the tie, concentrating the orange at the centre of the flowers. The paints will run into each other up to the gutta line which acts as a barrier.

5 Before the paints dry, sprinkle salt in small areas and then leave the tie to dry. The salt will draw out the paint and create a speckled effect. Leave for about 2 hours and then brush off the salt.

6 Brush colour over the back of the tie and let the shades run into each other.

7 Leave to dry once more and iron fix by pressing over a cloth on the wrong side of the tie with the iron set at a medium temperature.

For the Mosaic Tie
Materials
White silk tie
Water-based gutta (*gold*)
Silk paints (*red, blue, yellow, green, orange*)
Paintbrush (*fine*)

1 With the gold gutta draw a network of small squares and rectangles all over the front of the tie. Keep the lines as fine as possible as they may spread when you iron fix the tie. It's best to start at the end furthest away from you to prevent your arm brushing the wet gutta. Leave to dry.

2 Fill in the spaces with paints straight from the jars using the fine paintbrush. (If you get any runs you can re-divide the areas with the gutta when the paint is dry.) Leave to dry and then paint a mixture of colours freely on the back of the tie letting the shades run into each other.

3 Leave to dry once more and iron fix by pressing over a cloth on the wrong side of the tie with the iron set at a medium temperature.

Fleur de Lis Waistcoat

The Fleur de lis motif adds sophistication to any garment. Here I've used it to decorate a plain grey natural silk waistcoat.

Materials
Lightweight cardboard
Tracing paper
Pencil
Craft knife
Natural silk waistcoat
Disappearing pen
Dressmaker's pins
Water-based guttas (gold, silver)
Silk paint (blue)
Paintbrush (medium)

1 Trace the template on page 88 and then transfer it onto cardboard and cut it out with the craft knife (see Transferring Images on page 11).

2 Open out the waistcoat over a towel. With the dressmaker's pins, mark positions for the motif on the waistcoat so that they are evenly spaced. Place the cut-out into position over the pins and draw around the shape using the disappearing pen.

3 Starting at the top of the waistcoat (the edge furthest from you), draw over the pen lines in gutta using gold and silver for alternate motifs.

4 When the gutta is completely dry, paint in the outlines using the silk paint straight from the jar, but sparingly.

5 Leave to dry once more and iron fix by pressing on the wrong side of the tie with the iron set at a medium temperature.

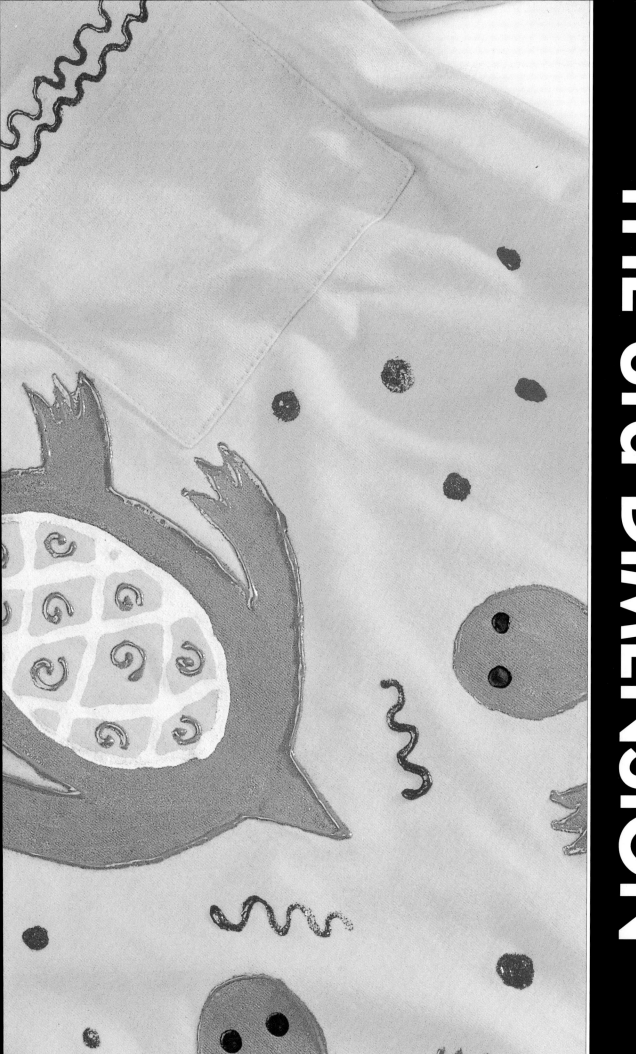

TECHNIQUES

In this chapter, I show you how to use many of the marvellous techniques that add three-dimensional effects to your clothes. Whether you choose to use paints, studs or embroider with ribbons, there is something here for you.

Three-dimensional paints

A number of companies now produce painting products that will give you a shiny three-dimensional effect. These paints are intended for use on just about anything from tin cans to fabric. Miraculously, they are self-fixing and washable, although one shouldn't put garments painted with them in a tumble-dryer.

These paints are particularly good for children as they squeeze out from the bottle directly onto your fabric. They come in an endless range of colours from neon brights to copper tones and some of them have pearlized and glitter finishes. The beauty of these paints is that they can be used for both bold and delicate designs. You can produce tiny glistening pearls or big bold scribbles.

Because the paint is thick and has a plasticity, you can stick rhinestones and sequins directly onto it and it will hold them in position. You can also make mock beads by squeezing the paint in little blobs onto your fabric or you can use them as pens for lettering. The method is simple. The bottles have very fine nozzles that you hold just above your fabric. You then squeeze gently moving your hand in the direction you wish to go. Paints with very fine nozzles can also be used as an embroidery substitute — squeeze out the paint into little crosses to resemble cross stitch.

Puffy paints are also available. Apply them as above but when you have finished painting, dry them with a hairdryer or iron them on the back so the paint puffs up, giving a flocked effect.

When you are applying fabric paint direct from the bottle, make sure you don't smudge the paint with your hand.

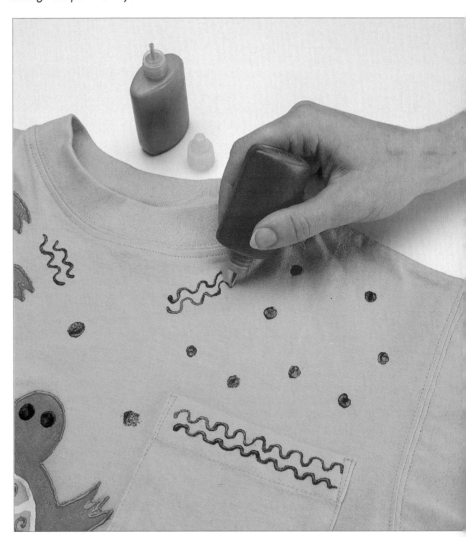

Three-dimensional paint (see page 56).

Ribbon embroidery (see right).

Three-dimensional fish (see page 59).

TECHNIQUE FOCUS:
Ribbon Embroidery

This is one of my favourite pastimes. With the introduction of a wonderful range of subtly coloured narrow silk ribbons, I've discovered that a few knots and loops strategically placed on a garment can make any non-stitcher appear to be the embroiderer of the year. When choosing your needle, check that the eye is large enough to take the ribbon freely.

Materials
Garment
Needle
Silk ribbons
Scissors

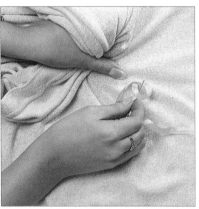

1 To make ribbon knots, bring the needle up through the fabric from the back of the garment. Wrap the ribbon around the needle once to form a knot close to the fabric.

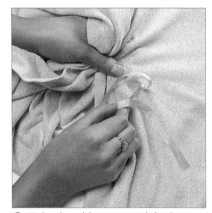

2 Take the ribbon around the knot and insert it as near as you can to your starting point. You now have a knot of ribbon with a coil of ribbon wrapped around it.

1 To make a daisy stitch, bring the threaded needle up through the fabric at the position that will form the centre of the first flower.

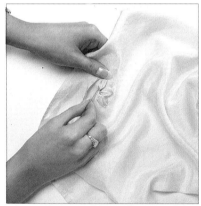

2 Make a small loop the size of the first petal, and put the needle back through the entry point holding the loop in place with your left hand.

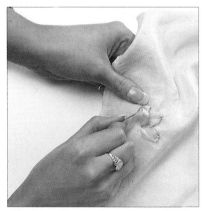

3 Bring the needle up just under the end of the loop and down again over the loop, catching it into position. Bring the needle back through at the centre of the flower. Repeat in a circle to form six petals.

53

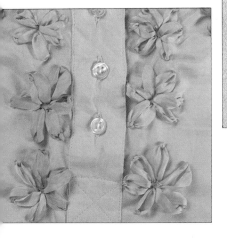

For the Silk Daisy Top
Materials
30in (75cm) lengths of ⅜in (7mm)-
wide silk ribbons (*pastel shades*)
Crewel needle (*for silk or cotton*) or
a tapestry needle (*for heavier fabrics
or knitwear*)

1 Mark the position on the top where
you want your daisies to fall. You
might choose to edge a neckline or
cuff, or scatter them randomly over a
plain garment.

2 Thread the needle and stitch each
daisy as described in the Technique
Focus on the previous page.

Silk Ribbon-embroidered Tops

These embroidered tops are worked with small knots and daisy stitch. Silk ribbons can be stitched on knitwear, cotton or silk. The success depends upon your choice of colours.

For the Lupin Top
Materials
Silk top
Greaseproof or parchment paper, or tracing paper
Pencil
Transfer pencil
Iron and ironing board
1yd (1m) each of ⅛in (4mm)-wide silk ribbons (*grey mauve, mauve, pink, red, wine*)
1yd (1m) each of ¹⁄₁₂in (2mm)-wide silk ribbons (*green, yellow*)
Crewel needle
Scissors

---

1 Trace the outline on page 90 onto the greaseproof or parchment paper, or tracing paper, and use the transfer pencil and iron to position it on the tee-shirt (see Transferring Images on page 11).

2 Where the knots are indicated on the template, make knots using the wider ribbon, as shown in the Technique Focus on the previous page. If you are an embroiderer, use french knots instead. Work the knots where indicated using the colours shown.

3 Work the leaves in backstitch using the narrower ribbons. Both the stems and the upper leaf are green, the lower leaf is stitched in yellow.

55

Thomas Turtle Tee-shirt

This eye-catching tee-shirt will be a colourful addition to any child's summer wardrobe - and the beauty is that it's simple and cheap to make. Just buy an inexpensive plain tee-shirt and jazz it up with this lively turtle design. Not only is the end result truly unique, it's great fun to make as well!

Materials
Prewashed tee-shirt
Cardboard
Greaseproof or parchment paper, or tracing paper
Transfer pencil
Iron and ironing board
Glossy fabric paints (*green, red, black*)
Saucer
Paintbrush
Puff fabric paint (*white*)
Glitter fabric paint (*red*)

1 Place a piece of cardboard between the front and back of the tee-shirt to keep the surface taut and to stop the paint going through to the back. Trace the outline on page 92 onto the greaseproof or parchment paper, or tracing paper, and use the transfer pencil and iron to position it on the tee-shirt (see Transferring Images on page 11).

2 Squeeze some green paint into a saucer and fill in the green areas on the template using a paintbrush. Leave to dry and then add the other outlines as shown on the motif, applying the paint straight from the bottles.

3 Add the squiggles and dots which surround the turtle, alternately using the glitter red and glossy red fabric paints.

4 Repeat the turtle and squiggles and dots randomly over the tee-shirt. Dry thoroughly overnight then iron over the back of the tee-shirt to make the white paint puff up and also to fix all the paints. Leave for at least 72 hours before washing.

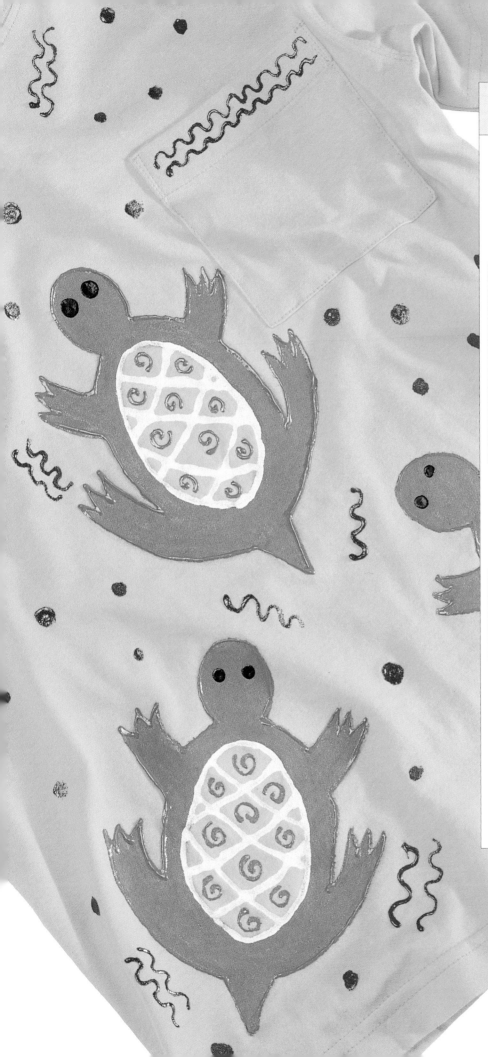

TECHNIQUE FOCUS:
Applying a Template
and Fabric Paints

Materials
Tee-shirt
Transfer pencil
Greaseproof or parchment paper, or
tracing paper
Iron and ironing board
Fabric paints

1 To transfer a template, go over
the outline with a transfer pencil
on the back of greaseproof or
parchment paper, or tracing
paper. Then position the outline
on your garment and lightly iron
over it.

2 Fabric paints which are sold in
bottles with nozzles are ideal for
drawing with. Simply draw
freehand or trace over previously
drawn lines.

57

Peter Penguin

Hand-me-downs are
no fun, especially if
you happen to be the
youngest in a family
of seven. So, why
not give kids' jeans a
completely new lease
of life with this
happy penguin?

Materials
Jeans or trousers
Pearl fabric paint (*white*)
Puff fabric paints (*white, black,
fluorescent orange*)
Paintbrush

Follow the instructions for Thomas Turtle
(see pages 56–7) but use the template
on page 91. As with Thomas, fill in large
areas of colour with a paintbrush and
use puff paint straight from the bottle for
the outlines. After making the large
penguin on the front of the trousers, add
fish details to the belt loops and on any
pockets or the bib, if there is one.

Goldfish Sweatshirt

The sweatshirt featured on this page and the bowler hat overleaf have been designed to wear together, but you may choose to decorate just one or the other of the pair - the choice is yours.

Materials
Tracing paper
Cardboard
Scissors
Tailor's chalk
Liquid glitter fabric paint (*gold*)
Paintbrushes (*medium, fine*)
Slick fabric paints (*black, red*)
Pearl fabric paints (*copper, green*)

1 Trace the templates on page 88 and then cut them out (see Transferring Images on page 11).

2 Lay the templates in position on the sweatshirt and draw around them with tailor's chalk. The top and second fishes are both size 2, and the three below are one each of sizes 3, 4 and 5.

3 Squeeze some of the glitter paint into a saucer and paint in the main body of the fishes with the medium paintbrush. Leave to dry.

4 Using the template as a guide and squeezing the paint directly from the bottle, add the back and tail fins in black slick fabric paint, the body fins in copper pearl fabric paint, the mouths in red slick fabric paint, and the eyeballs in green pearl fabric paint. Leave to dry, then outline the eyes in black and add the pupils. Finally, add the squiggly lines at the end of the tails in copper. Put little blobs of glitter where dots appear on the template.

59

Goldfish Bowler Hat

Brighten up last season's tired old hat to create your own individual style. This fishy design — designed to accompany the sweatshirt on the previous page — is painted on an old bowler, but really any dark hat made from a stiff material will do.

Materials
Tracing paper
Cardboard
Scissors
Tailor's chalk
Liquid glitter fabric paint (*gold*)
Paintbrushes (*medium, fine*)
Slick fabric paints (*black, red*)
Pearl fabric paints (*copper, green*)

1 Follow steps 1 to 4 for decorating the Goldfish Sweatshirt on the previous page. But place fish 1 on the top of the hat, four size 2 fishes around the crown, and one size 3 fish on the centre front of the brim.

2 At the end, add the bubbles coming from the fishes' mouths in the gold glitter fabric paint. Put small blobs of glitter on the bubbles at the same time as adding them to the fishes' bodies.

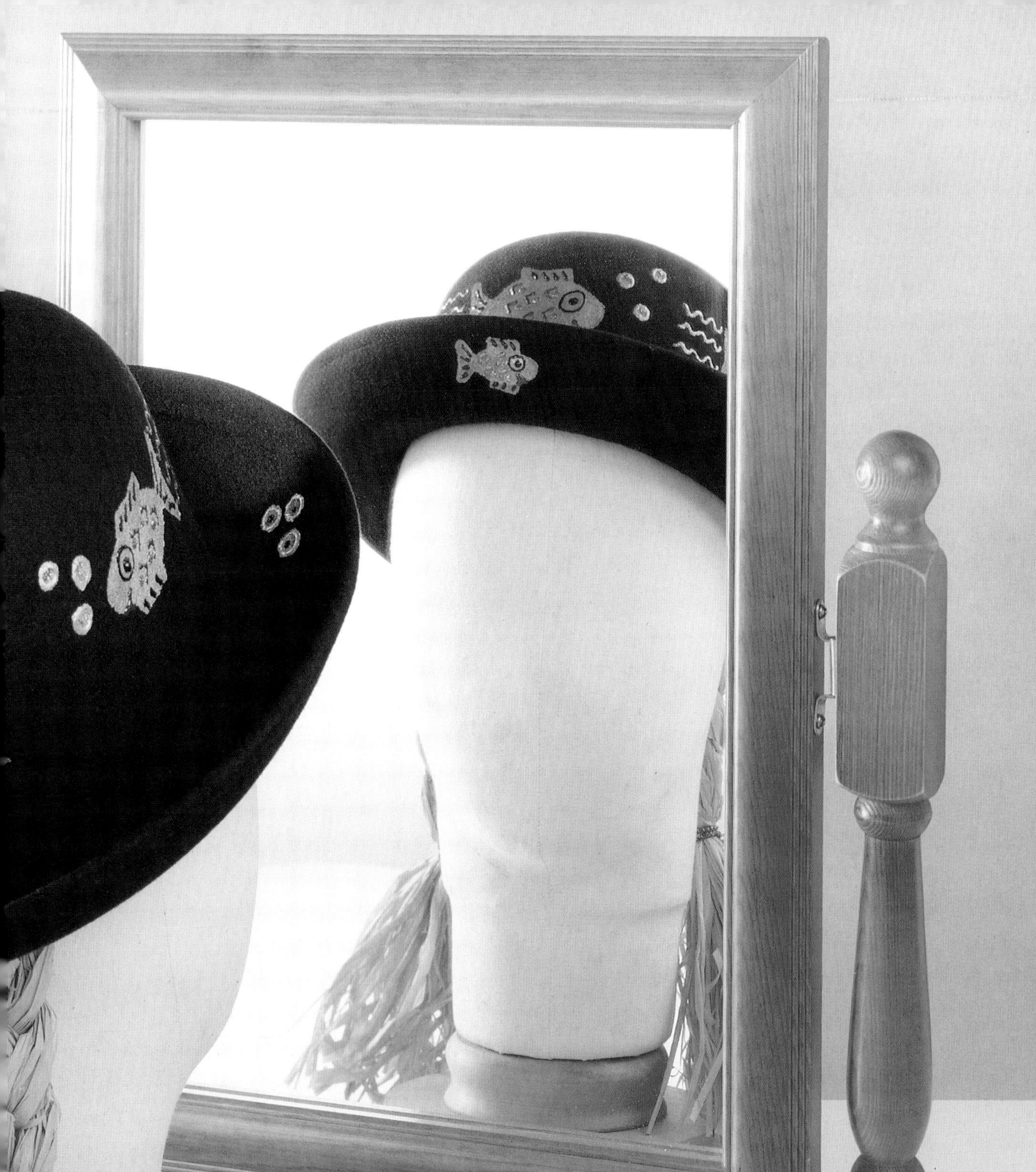

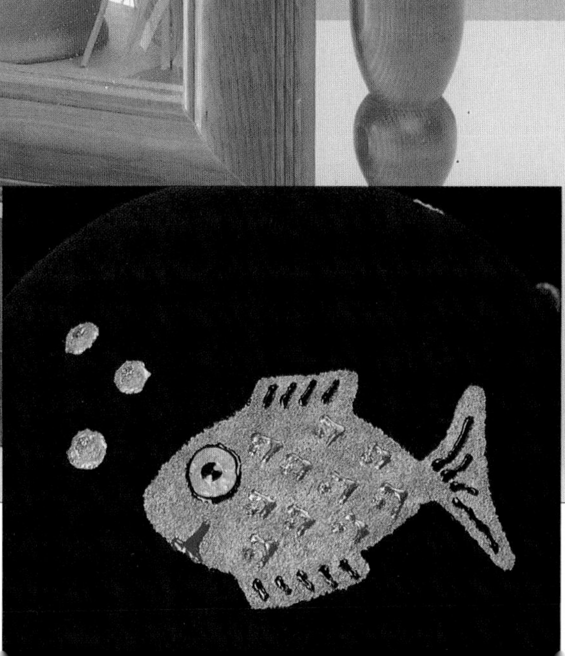

These Boots are Made for

Here are three very simple ways of turning cheap pairs of canvas shoes into something special.

1 Dilute the transparent paint so that it is one part paint to two parts water and brush it quickly over the shoes with a broad paintbrush.

2 Dry and fix the paint with a hairdryer.

3 Copy the template on page 88 on the front of the shoes using the pencil.

4 Squeezing the paint straight from the bottle, paint in the flower head in pearl white and the stems and leaves in glossy green. Leave to dry.

alking

1 Paint the shoes with the fabric paint and fix it in place with the iron set on cotton.

2 Draw on the leaves freehand with the pencil and then go over the lines with the transfer glue. Leave to set and then add the gold foil (see Technique Focus, page 35).

3 Replace the laces with lengths of lace-trimmed ribbon. To stop the ribbon fraying, seal the ends with the transfer glue.

1 Draw the hearts on freehand using the pencil and then go over them squeezing the paint straight from the bottle.

2 If there are any tears, stains, marks or burns in the boots, fill in the appropriate hearts to cover them up. Use a hairdryer to fix the paint.

63

Pearl Jacket

This plain cream jacket hung unworn in a wardrobe for months. But then with the help of some three-dimensional paints it was turned into a real eye-catcher.

1 Sharpen your transfer pencil to a fine point.

2 Draw a row of dots around the right-hand front neckline of the jacket, each one approximately ½in (12mm) apart. Dot in a second row ¼in (6mm) down but in between the existing dots. Repeat the first and second rows.

3 Holding the light gold paint applicator directly above the first dot, but not touching the fabric, squeeze out a small blob of paint. (Practise first on some surplus material, it is all too easy to squeeze out an excess amount.) Complete the top row in light gold, the second row in dark gold, the third row in copper, and the fourth row in light gold.

4 Repeat steps 2 and 3 on the left-hand neckline.

5 If your jacket has pocket flaps decorate these in the same pattern.

6 Finally, add a few light gold random dots to the body of the jacket and the pockets.

7 Leave to dry for 72 hours, after which the paint is machine washable - but check the fabric care instructions before washing.

Materials
Transfer pencil
Round-necked jacket
Three-dimensional paints (*light gold,*
dark gold, copper)

TECHNIQUES

For this section, I have concentrated on using up bits and bobs left over from the main projects and doing up some jumble sale finds such as a small black plastic shoulder bag and a plain straw hat. I have also chosen to recycle old clothes found at the same jumble sales. For centuries, people have been mending their clothes with patches. This used to be strictly a method of repair but today sewing pieces of fabric onto a garment has become something of an art form, sometimes referred to as appliqué.

No-sew appliqué

Appliqué can be as simple or as complicated as you wish and with the introduction of fusible webbing materials you don't even need to be able to sew. Fusible webbing acts as a sheet of fabric glue. Trace the design onto both the fabric you are applying, and the webbing. Iron the webbing into position, peel off the paper backing and then iron on the fabric patch. If you have raw edges, these can be covered with a decorative row of top stitching.

Your own creation

To create the most artistic and original effects on your clothing the number one rule is to never throw anything out. The

following projects have been made from old bits of clothing varying from an old ethnic bag cut into strips and used as patches, to a black cotton bra which now looks positively Madonna-like. Fine fabrics such as laces and chiffons make great inserts and can transform a dowdy old skirt into magical partywear. Ribbons which are now available in a huge range of designs and textures can be stitched down the front of a garment in rows to give a striped effect. Bows can be sewn on to hide tears and stains.

Your selection of fabrics will provide the key to success. Unlikely colours can sit well together and your choice is really a matter of trial and error. It is a good idea to use colours in a similar tone range and for this purpose, I divide my scraps into four bags labelled Summer, Winter, Autumn and Spring, and group fabrics together that will fit into these categories.

Before beginning a design, it is a good idea to draw a rough sketch of the shape of your garment and to cut a lot of random shapes from coloured paper. Arrange the paper shapes onto your sketch to give yourself a basic plan and a feel for the overall look and balance of the arrangement. You can, of course, use fabric trims together with paint effects (see the Lace-trimmed Top on page 74 for a three-dimensional look). The most

Hand-made ribbon roses (see page 79).

Ribbon trims (see page 78).

Bejewelled bag (see page 80).

Appliquéd poodle mac (see page 85).

TECHNIQUE FOCUS:
Sewing on Patches

If you are handy with a needle and thread you can cut out and apply fabric shapes to your garments using various methods. If you have a sewing machine, the simplest method is to pin the shape into position and to sew around the edges in buttonhole stitch. You can also do this by hand although it is quite labour intensive.

The method used to apply fabric shapes in quilting is to trace the design onto the fabric and then cut out the piece allowing a selvage of about ½in

(12mm) all around the edge. Clip the selvage with a pair of small pointed scissors, fold under the fabric and baste it in place, leaving smooth edges and curves. Then sew it to your garment using a blind hem stitch.

You can also stitch the fabric patch onto your garment with fancy embroidery stitches such as chain stitch. If you use a bright coloured contrasting embroidery thread this will add to the overall effect of your design.

important thing is to create something that you like: this is your statement and it does not matter what anyone else thinks.

Studding

Studs can be purchased from department and craft stores in a great variety of shapes and sizes, along with special applicators and full details on how to attach them. A basic stud has claws at the back which grip onto your fabric and the applicator provides the means for

closing these claws. If you intend doing a lot of studding, it would be wise to invest in a studding machine which has adjustable fitments that you change according to the size of the stud you wish to use. Studding machines will work on most fabrics, including leather, but do not apply studs to very fine fabric because they are quite weighty.

Rhinestones and gemstones are equally easy to buy and use. They will adhere to three-dimensional paints as well as undecorated fabrics, so use the paints to create a setting for your stone.

69

Appliquéd

Woollen Waistcoat

This man's woollen waistcoat has been transformed using traditional hand stitched appliqué, embellished with an unusual mix of fabrics including Indian mirror work, velvet, paisley brushed cotton, and floral fabrics cut from old curtains.

Materials
Waistcoat
Selection of fabric remnants
Scissors
Pins
Sewing machine
Cotton thread
Needle
Beads
Buttons

Read the sections on Your own Creation and Sewing on Patches on pages 68 and 69, and you will have a clear idea of how to create something similar yourself. The art is in the selection of fabrics and it is this that will turn your project into a personal statement.

Notice how leaf shapes have been cut from an old leather jacket and added to the front points of the waistcoat to add texture, and beads and buttons have also been scattered over the waistcoat.

Decorated Denim

This denim waistcoat is an example of how simple appliqué can transform a garment. The waistcoat was bought at a rummage sale along with a very tatty bag of ethnic Indian origin.

Materials

Denim waistcoat
Indian bag
Scissors
Pins
Sewing machine
Cotton thread
Needle (*optional*)
Sheels (*optional*)
Beads (*optional*)

1 Cut the bag into strips and squares.

2 Arrange on the waistcoat and then pin in place once you have decided what looks best.

3 Machine-stitch into place using a close zigzag stitch.

4 On the back of the waistcoat a long strip of bag has been stitched down the centre. Since the waistcoat ends in a point at the centre back, the end of the strip has also been cut into a point to follow the line.

5 If you want to add more features to the design you could stitch on some shells or beads around the armholes and neckline.

Lilac Lamé Tee-shirt

A pair of old fifties' curtains, a handful of buttons and a touch of lamé have transformed this simple lilac sleeveless tee-shirt into a designer original.

Materials

Sleeveless tee-shirt
12in (*30cm*) square piece of cotton printed fabric
Sewing machine or
needle and cotton thread
8 x 4in (*20 x 10cm*) piece of lamé
6 buttons (*assorted*)

1 Using the templates on page 92 (if necessary, enlarge them on a photocopier to an appropriate size), cut out two fabric shapes from the printed cotton.

2 Position and pin these to the front of the tee-shirt, turning under the selvage as you go. Machine or hand stitch into place.

3 Fold the lamé in half lengthwise, with right sides facing. Stitch the two long edges together and turn right sides out. Stitch a row of running stitches down the centre of the doubled length of fabric, and gather by pulling gently on the thread. Stitch into position at the left side of the neckline.

4 Take the buttons and stitch them to the tee-shirt using the photograph to the left as a guide for positioning.

5 For the back, try varying the shapes of the appliqué.

73

Lace and Fabric Trimmed Tops

These little ribbed tops were bought from a street market. Add some lace trim and a dash of fabric paint or stick on strips and squares of fabrics, and they are quite transformed.

For the Lace-trimmed Top
Materials
2yd (2m) of 1¼in (3cm)-wide white lace with raised pattern
Fabric pens (*magenta, yellow, green*)
White top
Fabric glue or needle and cotton thread (*white*)
3 small white buttons
Small white ribbon bow

1 Highlight flowers or areas of patterning on the lace with the fabric pens.

2 Cut two lengths of lace long enough to fit down the front of the top and glue or stitch them into position, turning the bottom edge to the inside of the hem.

3 Cut a length of lace long enough to fit around the hem. Glue or stitch in place.

4 If the lace has a fancy narrow edging, trim this from a length and glue or stitch it around the armholes and neckline.

5 Dab the buttons with your fabric pens and stitch between the two front panels of lace.

6 Dab paint onto a small bow and glue or stitch it into position above the buttons.

For the Fabric-trimmed Top
Materials
4½ x 6in (12 x 15cm) piece of cotton gingham
4½in (12cm) of ½in (12mm)-wide fusible webbing
4 buttons (*white*)
3 narrow satin bows (*black*)

1 Pin the gingham and the fusible webbing together and cut four 2¼in (5.5cm) squares through both layers.

2 Arrange the webbing squares on your garment and iron into position. Peel off the paper backing.

3 Place the gingham squares over the webbing and iron into position.

4 Cut two narrow strips of webbing and fabric, each 4½in (12cm) long, and press down centre front using the method described in steps 2 and 3. Add a small strip of fabric across the bottom to join the two vertical pieces.

5 Stitch the buttons between the vertical strips of fabric alternating them with the satin bows.

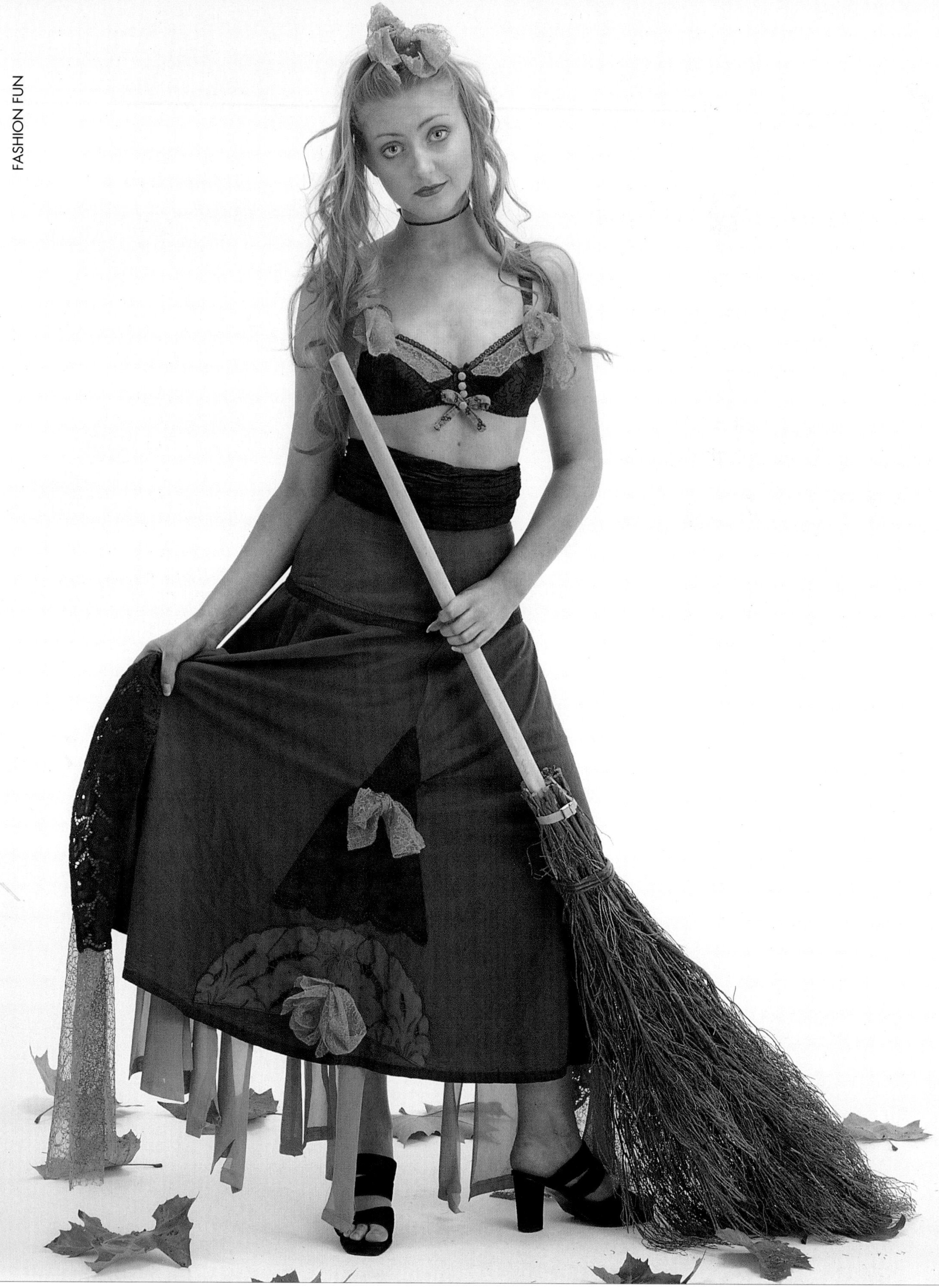

Cinderella's Ballgown

Yes, you shall go to the ball, but you will obviously not be able to lay your hands on the exact pieces of fabric and old dresses used in this design. So, after reading the instructions, experiment with your own remnants. Die fabrics in advance, if necessary.

Materials

For the Skirt
Cotton skirt (*black*)
Cutwork doily (*black*)
lace dress bodice with zip up the back (*black*)
½yd (½m) lace (*pink*)
Nylon petticoat (*pink*)

For the Bra
Bra (*black*)
Lace remnant (*pink*)
Piece of broderie anglaise (*eyelet*) (*black*)
Cotton threads (*black, pink*)
Needle
4 small cloth-covered buttons

Making the skirt

1 Cut the doily in half and stitch one half to the bottom centre front of the skirt and the other half to the bottom centre back.

2 Take the lace dress bodice and separate the front from the back. Unpick and remove the zip. The back is now in two halves.

3 From the front of the bodice cut a triangle of lace and stitch it to the centre front of the skirt, above the doily.

4 Cut two lengths of pink lace measuring approximately 12 x 24in (30 x 61cm) and stitch one short end halfway up the side of the skirt, overlapping the side seam. Repeat for the other side.

5 Make three pink lace bows from pieces of lace measuring 3 x 12in (7.5 x 30cm). Stitch one to the centre bottom of each half doily, and the third on the triangle of lace at the bottom front of the skirt, about 10in (25cm) above the other pink bow on the front.

6 Stitch the two black lace bodice back halves into position over the lace on the side seams so that the shoulder edges of what was the bodice dangle down.

7 Take the petticoat and cut it into panels. Stitch it to the inside of the skirt so the panels hang approximately 12in (30cm) below the hemline.

Decorating the bra

1 Cut two 1in (2.5cm) strips of pink lace and stitch in place to form a 'V' at the front of the bra.

2 Make two pink lace bows and tie them to the bra straps.

3 Cut a length of broderie anglaise and tie it in a bow, and then stitch it to the bottom of the bra in the centre.

4 Cover four small buttons with pink lace and stitch them down the front of the bra placing the last one in the centre of the broderie angliase bow.

Ribboned Hat

This hat has been decorated with a variety of leftover ribbons and three different techniques, each of which can be applied to all sorts of different items of clothing.

1 Rouche a wide length of ribbon. Cut a length to fit around the hat one and a half times. Dot the brim of the hat at intervals with fabric glue and scrunch the ribbon, catching it into position on the glued areas.

2 Add some curled ribbons. To do this pull a length of ribbon along a pair of scissors.

3 Finally, dot ribbon roses all over the brim. To make the roses, see the Technique Focus to the right.

TECHNIQUE FOCUS:
Making Ribbon Roses

Once you have mastered the technique, ribbon roses are very easy to make, and quick too.

Materials
Florist's wire
Ribbon
Scissors

1 Take a length of wire and fold it in two. Twist it together to form a stem, leaving a 2in (5cm) loop at the top.

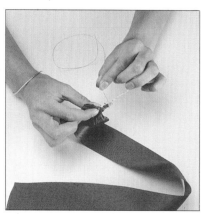

2 Take the ribbon and wind it around itself two or three times to form the centre of the flower. Cut another length of wire and wrap it around the bottom of the rose to secure.

3 Continue to make the rest of the rose by alternating folding it around the centre and back on itself, all the time securing it by wrapping more of the wire around the base.

4 Finish off the rose by securely wrapping wire around the bottom.

5 You can make roses in all kinds of ribbons, from fine organzas to heavy plaids, depending on the look you want for your hat.

Novel Neckwear and Bag

Here are two necklaces and a bag made from string, feathers and other odds and ends that were just lying about.

For the String Necklace
Materials
1yd (1m) of string (*the hairy kind*)
Fabric paints (*purple, green, silver*)
Paintbrush
Florist's wire
Remnants of lace and raffia
Old-fashioned clothes' peg
Acrylic gemstone
Wood glue

1 Take the length of string and knot it two or three times at regular intervals to form decorative balls. Then paint over the string and knots in sections of purple and green.

2 Wind the florist's wire around the length of the necklace. Fold one end of the string back on itself to form a loop and secure it with wire. Wrap plenty of wire around the other end of the string so that when folded back on itself it is stiff enough to form a hook.

3 Take a narrow length of lace and tie short bits of raffia onto it so they look like bows. Cross the lace over and under a section of the string and secure it with a knot behind one of the string knots. Repeat for other side of the necklace.

4 Paint the clothes' peg in a mixture of purple, green and silver. When dry, decorate it with wire, stick the coloured bead onto the top, and slot the peg onto the necklace.

For the Feather and Leather Necklace
Materials
1½yd (1½m) leather thong
14 feathers
All-purpose adhesive
Remnants of silk embroidery threads
Blunt sewing needle

1 Take the leather thong and tie seven, equally spaced, knots in it. Fold the knotted thong in half and knot the ends together — this forms the bottom of the necklace.

2 Take two feathers and glue them just below a knot, then bind them with silk embroidery thread threaded through the needle. Weave the silk back through the binding to secure the ends. Repeat beneath each knot.

For the Bejewelled Bag
Materials
Small leather or plastic bag
Fabric paint (*silver*)
Paintbrush
PVA glue or standard white glue
4 acrylic gemstones

1 Apply the fabric paint over the surface of the bag with the paintbrush — the reaction of the paint on the leather/plastic provides the marbling effect.

2 Highlight any raised areas such as buckles and straps by leaving them unpainted. Leave paint to dry and then decorate further by gluing on gemstones.

Navy Studded Shirt...

...and Kid's Hat

A simple navy shirt and kid's denim hat take on a new lease of life with the addition of a few studs. Studs can be used in conjunction with painted images or to highlight an appliquéd design so don't limit yourself to the ideas on these pages.

Materials
Shirt
Hat
Chalk
Enamel fabric paint (red)
(for the hat only)
Paintbrush (for the hat only)
Studs (assorted shapes and sizes)
Stud applicator

---

1 Mark out the positions of your studs with a piece of chalk first. Once you have determined the basic design, shop around for different shapes of stud to suit your design. On this shirt I highlighted the collar and tops of the pockets with a mixture of round, hexagonal and star-shaped studs.

2 For the kid's hat, dilute the fabric paint in a saucer with a few drops of water and then apply it with a paintbrush. Leave to dry before adding the studs.

3 Fix them in place following the manufacturer's instructions (see Studding, page 69).

83

Poodle Rain

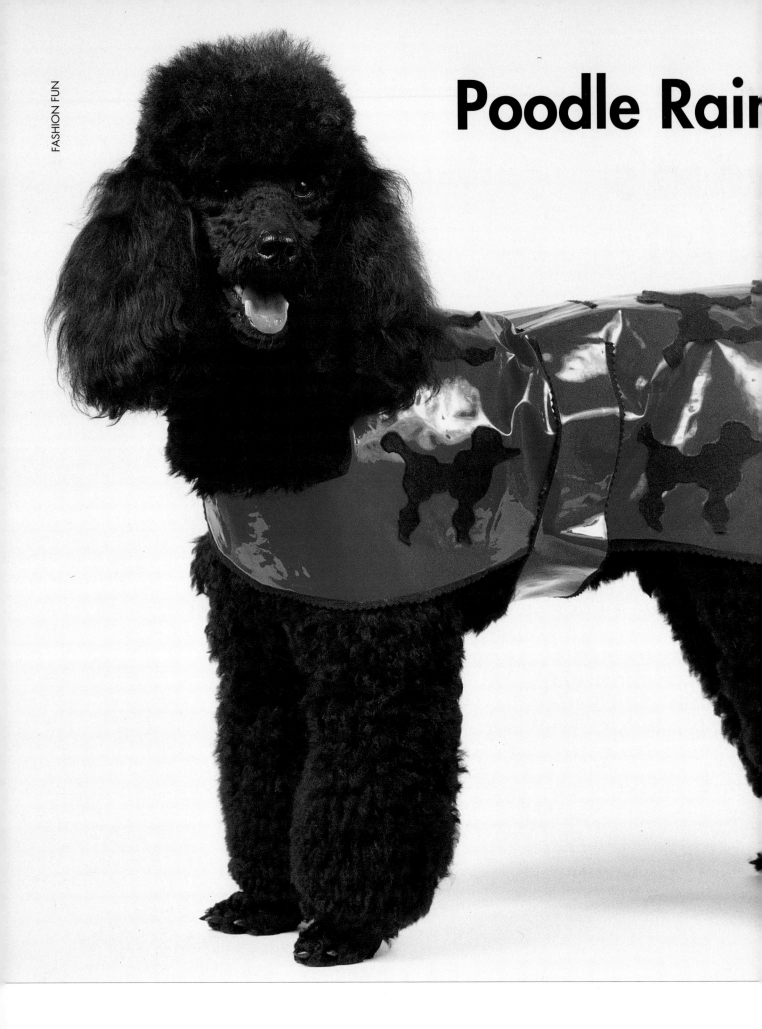

Mac

I simply couldn't complete this book without including something in it for my best friend. Not least of all because if ignored, she might just bite off my arm. This raincoat is suitable for any miniature-sized dog.

Materials
Tracing paper
Pencil
Brown paper
Scissors
30in (76cm)-square piece of felt (black)
Tailor's chalk
Pinking shears
24in (61cm)-square piece of vinyl (red)
Felt-tip pen
PVA glue or standard white glue
4in (10cm) strip of touch-and-close fastener or 2 sets of touch-and-close dots

1 Work out the correct size for your mac by measuring the length of the dog's back and around his/her stomach. Adjust the shaping on the body using the template on page 93 as a guide and make the waistband 3in (7.5cm) longer than your dog's stomach measurement, to allow for the overlap which carries the velcro fastening.

2 Enlarge the template on page 93 on a photocopier to a suitable size for your dog's measurements. Trace the outlines and cut out a paper pattern from the brown paper.

3 Lay the paper pattern onto the black felt and draw around it with the tailor's chalk. Cut out the main body and the band with the pinking shears.

4 Cut off ½in (12mm) all around the paper pattern. Place the amended cut-out onto the vinyl and draw around this with the felt-tip pen. Cut out both pieces with the scissors.

5 Glue the vinyl body over the felt lining so that the pinked edges show. Do the same with the band and then glue the band over the narrowest width of the coat.

6 Overlap the ends of the waistband and glue touch-and-close pieces or dots into corresponding positions at each end of the band so they fit comfortably when slightly overlapped. (Ask your dog to tell you when the band feels comfortable.) Do the same with the neck area, placing one side of the touch-and-close fastener on the felt side (right-hand side of neck) and the other on the vinyl side (left-hand side of neck). (Don't strangle the dog unless you really want to.)

7 Enlarge and make a paper pattern of the poodle outline on page 93 as in step 2. If you need help with making a different outline, trace one from a dog book.

8 Lay your pattern on the remaining black felt and draw around the outline with the tailor's chalk. Carefully cut out the image eight times. Arrange these around the coat and glue down with PVA glue or standard white glue.

Happy Sun Tee-shirt (see pages 26–7)

———————— gold glitter paint

Pink Daisy Canvas Shoes (see page 62)

Goldfish Sweater and Bowler Hat (see pages 59–61)

rose leaves

Rose-stencilled Tee-shirt (see pages 22–3)

rose

88

Fleur de Lis Waistcoat (see pages 48–9)

Gutta Painted Tie (see pages 46–7)

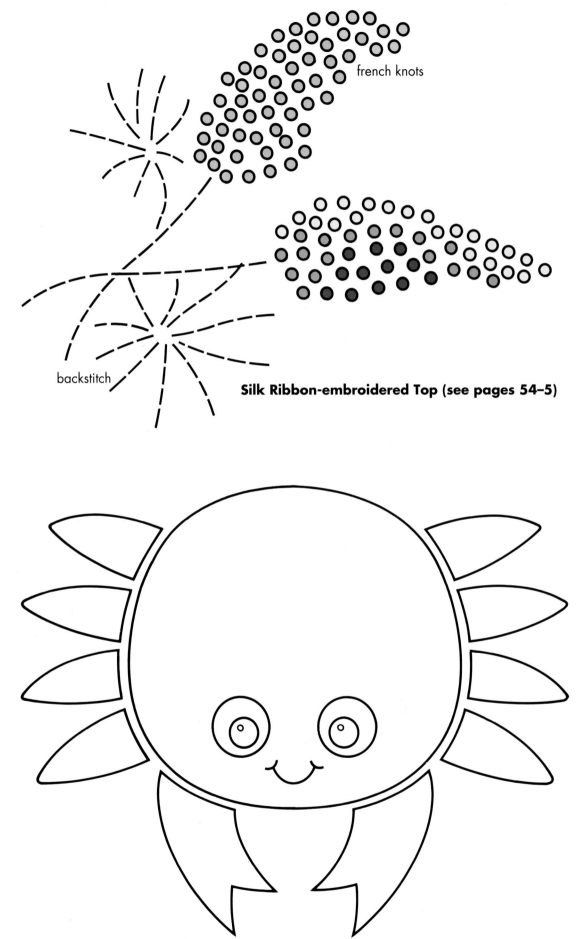

french knots

backstitch

Silk Ribbon-embroidered Top (see pages 54–5)

90 **Christopher the Crab (see page 24)**

Peter Penguin (see page 58)

pocket motif

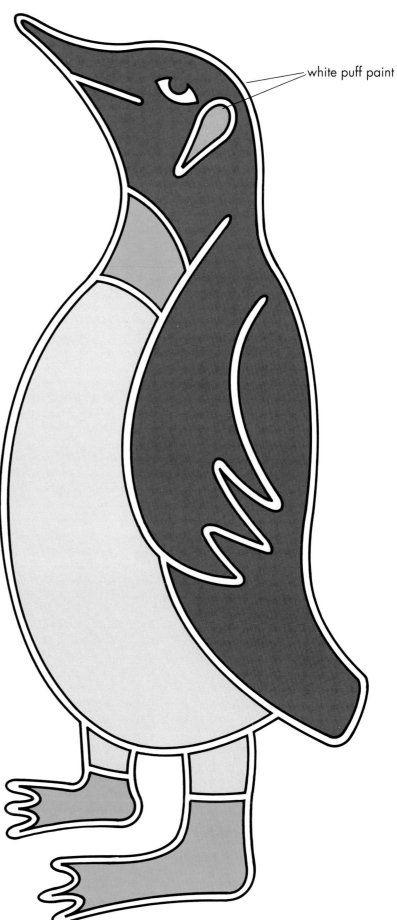

white puff paint

91

Thomas Turtle Tee-shirt (see pages 56–7)

white puff paint

Lilac Lamé Tee-shirt (see page 73)

Poodle Rain Mac (see pages 84–5)

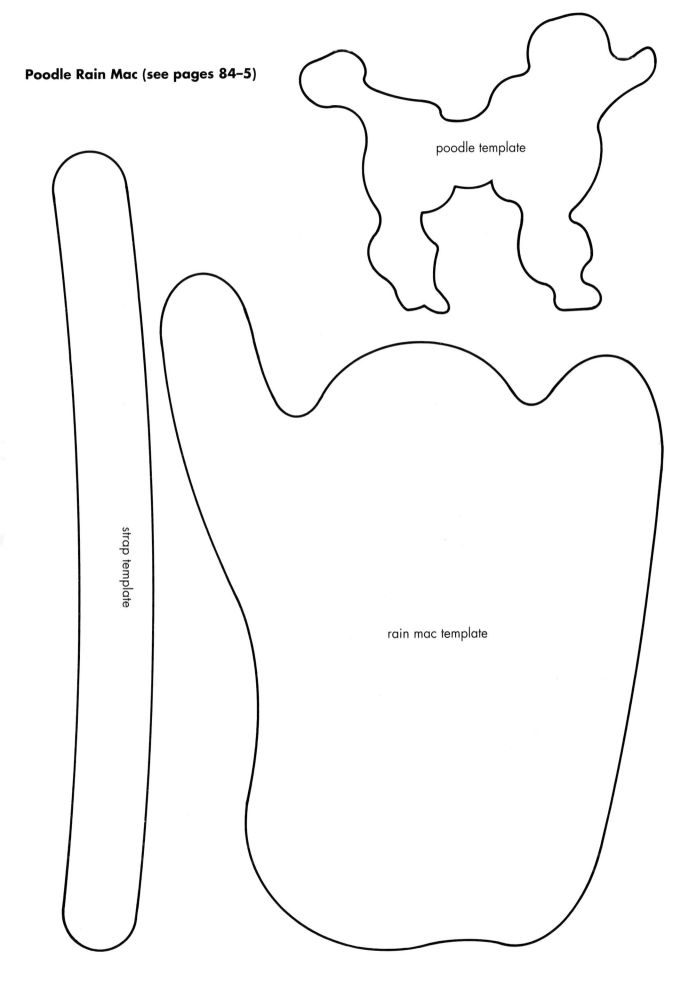

poodle template

strap template

rain mac template

93

Stockist Information

Many of the products in this book are interchangeable, but several manufacturers stand out in terms of quality and availability. Listed below are the products I used for each project, and this is followed by the companies' addresses and phone numbers to contact for stockist information.

pages 14-15:
BLUE SUNBURST TEE-SHIRT AND MARBLED SHORTS
Cold water dye: Dylon
Cold fix: Dylon

pages 16-17:
STRIPED TEE-SHIRT
Fabric paint: Pébéo Setacolor Transparent

pages 18-19:
SUN-FADING AND BLEACHING
Sun-faded tee-shirt
Transparent paint: Pébéo Setacolor Transparent

pages 20-21:
PHOTO TRANSFER TEE-SHIRT
Fabric paint: Dylon Colorfun
Transfer fluid: Dylon Image Maker

pages 22-3:
STENCILLED TEE-SHIRTS
Rose tee-shirt
Fabric paints: Jones Tones Paint
Alphabet tee-shirt
Fabric paints: Marabu Textil Paints
Fabric marker: Pébéo Setaskrib

page 24:
CHRISTOPHER THE CRAB
Fabric marker pen: Pébéo Setaskrib
Fabric paints: Marabu Textil Paints

page 25:
PATRICIA PARROT LEGGINGS
Fabric paints: Marabu Textil Paints

pages 26-7:
SUN AND STAR TEE-SHIRTS
Happy Sun tee-shirt
Fabric liner: Marabu Textil Magic-Liner
Fabric paints: Marabu Textil Paints
Glitter liner: Marabu Textil Glitter-Liner
Astral Star tee-shirt .
Felt-tip marker pens: Pébéo Setaskrib

pages 28-9:
WATERCOLOUR TUNIC
Silk paints: Deka

pages 30-1:
PAINTED LEATHER JERKIN
Fabric paints: Jones Tones Paints
Fabric liner: Marabu Textil Magic-Liner

pages 36-7:
PERMANENT JEWELRY
Transfer glue: Jones Tones Plexi 400
Transfer foils: Jones Tones Plexi Foils
Fabric glitter: Jones Tones Colour Dazzle
3-dimensional pearl fabric paints: Jones Tones Paint

pages 38-9:
GLITTER CATSUIT
Fabric glue: Jones Tones Plexi 400
Fabric glitter: Jones Tones Colour Dazzle
Glitter paint: Jones Glitter Tones

pages 40-1:
STARRY NIGHT HAT AND MATCHING BRA
Fabric glue: Jones Tones Plexi 400
Fabric glitter: Jones Tones Colour Dazzle
Glitter paint: Jones Glitter Tones

pages 42-3:
FLORAL POTATO-PRINT SARONG
Fabric paints: Marabu Textil Paints
3-dimensional Fabric paints: Dylon
Fabric glitter: Jones Tones Colour Dazzle

pages 44-5:
CHILD'S POTATO-PRINT SKIRT, TOP AND BAG
Fabric paints: Marabu Textil Paints
Fabric glitter: Jones Tones Colour Dazzle

pages 46-7:
GUTTA PAINTED TIES
Floral tie
Disappearing pen: Madeira Threads
Water-based gutta: Pébéo Setasilk
Silk paints: Deka
Mosaic tie
Water-based gutta: Pébéo Setasilk
Silk paints: Deka

pages 48-9:
FLEUR DE LIS WAISTCOAT
Disappearing pen: Madeira Threads
Water-based guttas: Pébéo Setasilk
Silk paint: Deka

pages 56-7:
THOMAS TURTLE TEE-SHIRT
All fabric paints: Dylon Colorfun

pages 58:
PETER PENGUIN
All fabric paints: Dylon Colorfun

pages 59:
GOLDFISH SWEATSHIRT
All fabric paints: Tulip Fabric Paints

pages 60-1:
GOLDFISH BOWLER HAT
All fabric paints: Tulip Fabric Paints

pages 62-3:
THESE BOOTS ARE MADE FOR WALKING
Pink daisy canvas shoes
Transparent paint: Pébéo Setacolor
All fabric paints: Dylon Colorfun
Red heart canvas boots
Glossy fabric paint: Dylon Colorfun
Gold leaf canvas shoes
Fabric paint: Marabu Textil Paint
Transfer glue: Jones Tones Plexi 400
Transfer foil: Jones Tones Plexi Foil

pages 64-5:
PEARL JACKET
3-dimensional paints: Tulip ColorPoint

pages 74-5:
LACE AND FABRIC TRIMMED TOPS
Lace trimmed top
Fabric pens: Pébéo Setaskrib

pages 76-7:
CINDERELLA'S BALLGOWN
Fabric paints: Jones Tones Paint

pages 80-1:
NOVEL NECKWEAR AND BAG
String necklace
Fabric paints: Jones Tones Paint
Bejewelled bag
Fabric paint: Marabu Textil Paint

pages 82-3:
NAVY STUDDED SHIRT AND KID'S HAT
Fabric paint: Jones Enamel Tones

Stockists and Suppliers

DEKA
Deka make my very favourite silk paints, plus a range of special-effect textile paints. They can be purchased in the UK by mail order from Atlascraft, in the US from Decart, and from Deka in Europe. Atlastcraft in the UK also sell a wide range of craft materials.

Atlascraft Ltd
Ludlow Hill Road
West Bridgford
Nottingham
NG2 6HD
Telephone: 01602 452202

Decart
PO Box 309
Morrisville
VT 05661
USA
Telephone: (802) 888 4217

Deka-Textilfarben GmbH
D-8025 Unterhaching
Germany
Telephone: 0 89/6 11 40 7 4

DYLON INTERNATIONAL
For dyes, look no further than Dylon International who manufacture an excellent range of products. For the tie-dying section we have used their cold dyes, but they also make machine-wash and hot-wash dyes in addition to selling a range of three-dimensional fabric paints in various finishes.

Dylon International Ltd
London SE26 5HE
Telephone: 0181 663 4801

Prymtritz
PO Box 5028
Spartanburg
SC 29304
USA
Telephone: (803) 576 5050

JONES TONES
These products are made in America and are wonderful for the creative clothes decorator. Their three-dimensional paints do not harden or crack and can therefore be used on stretchy as well as plain fabrics. The paints are available in a staggering range of colours and finishes, including glitter, pearl and enamel tones. They also produce a range of glitters in stunning colours and a unique foiling system (see Permanent Jewelry, page 36).

FW Bramwell & Co Ltd
Unit 5
Metcalf Drive
Altham Lane
Altham
Accrington
Lancs BB5 5TU
Telephone: 01282 779811

Jones Tones
68-743 Perez Road
D-16 Cathedral City
CA 92234
USA
Telephone: (800) 397 9667

MARABU TEXTIL PAINTS
Marabu Textil Paints have been used extensively in this book but in addition, this company produce an extensive range of effect paints which include specialized products for silk painters. Marabu are distributed in the UK by

Edding. Overseas readers should contact their head office in Germany for details on local distributors.

Edding (UK) Ltd
Edding House
Merlin Centre
Acrewood Way
St Albans
Herts AL4 0JY
Telephone: 01727 846688

Marabuwerke GmbH & Co
D-71730 Tamm
Germany
Telephone: 0 71 41/6 91-0

PHILIP AND TACEY
This company distribute a vast collection of items for the painter and textile artist. They are the main agents for Pébéo whose range includes Setacolor paints, Setaskrib pens, Setasilk transparent paints and Pébéo gutta pens. In addition, they stock a very inspiring range of silk clothing and accessories that are ready to paint and a collection of three-dimensional painting products.

Philip and Tacey Ltd
North Way
Andover
Hampshire SP10 5BA
Telephone: 01264 332171

Pébéo Canada
1035 St Denis
Sherbrooke, QC
J1K 2S7
Canada
Telephone: (819) 829 5012

TULIP
Another innovative manufacturer is Tulip whose three-dimensional paints are backed with leaflets that give you lots of ideas for using them. Their Colorpoint range is used to create liquid beads (see Pearl Jacket, page 64) and they also sell soft fabric paints in various finishes. Tulip are distributed by Inscribe in the UK.

Inscribe Ltd
The Woolmer Industrial Estate
Bordon
Hampshire GU35 9QE
Telephone: 01420 475747

Tulip
24 Prime Park Way
Natick
MA 01760
USA
Telephone: (508) 650 5400

W WILLIAMS & SON
W Williams & Son distribute a number of products that are ideal for the clothes decorator. Among them are Plaid three-dimensional paints and acrylic gemstones from The Beadery.

W Williams & Son
Regent House
1 Thane Villas
London N7 7PH
Telephone: 0171 263 7311

The Beadery
Greene Plastics Corporation
Hope Valley
RI 02832
USA
Telephone: (401) 539 2432

Miscellaneous

Disappearing pens are made by Madeira Threads (UK) Ltd. They are air- or water-soluble. The water-soluble version has an eraser at one end that you rub over your drawn line to make it disappear. Markings from the air-soluble pen disappear by themselves. For stockists, contact:

Madeira Threads (UK) Ltd
Thirsk Industrial Park
York Road
Thirsk
North Yorkshire
YO7 3BX
Telephone: 01845 524880

Madeira (USA) Ltd
PO Box 6068
30 Bayside Court
Laconia
NH 03246
Telephone: (603) 528 2944

For a huge variety of beads and also for studs and studding machines, you cannot do better than Creative Beadcraft who operate a mail-order service.

Creative Beadcraft
Denmark Works
Sheepcote Dell Road
Beamond End
Nr Amersham
Bucks HP7 0RX
Telephone: 01494 715606

Silk ribbons in various widths and numerous colours can be purchased by mail order from:

Ribbon Designs
42 Lake View
Edgware
Middx HA8 7RU
Telephone: 0181 958 4966

CM Offray & Son Ltd
Fir Tree Place
Church Road
Ashford
Middx TW15 2PH
Telephone: 01784 247281

For feathers, felts, hessian, beads, glues and raffia, write to Fred Aldous Ltd, who you will find to be extremely friendly and helpful. They sell exclusively by mail order. Alternatively, comb your local department store which stocks all these wonderful accessories.

Fred Aldous Ltd
37 Lever Street
Manchester 1
M60 1UX
Telephone: 0161 236 2477

For silk painting requisites, frames and blank ties, contact:

George Weil & Sons Ltd
The Warehouse
Reading Arch Road
Redhill
Surrey RH1 1HG
Telephone: 01737 778868

ACKNOWLEDGMENTS

For this book I was lucky enough to have the assistance of three very talented art students who came up with a wealth of original ideas and projects. I am therefore indebted to:
St Martin's College of Art, London, for Elena Symeou and Carmarthen College of Art, Dyfed, Wales, for Rhonda Davies and Carol Jones.
Two established designers who create and sell painted and recycled clothing for a living also produced garments that I couldn't resist using. The Fish bowler hat and sweatshirt (see pages 59–61) were created by Jacqui Kolbe who sells her wares through many designer shops and also at Camden Lock Market, London. The appliquéd waistcoats (see pages 70 and 72) and Lilac Lamé tee-shirt (see page 73) came from Jenny Long. She is a talented designer who specializes in recycling old clothes mostly purchased at rummage sales. Jenny sells to private customers and at craft fairs. You can reach her at 14 Clairmont Road, Lexden, Colchester, Essex XO3 5BE. My thanks also to Mary Day for her sun-faded top (see page 18) (Mary also produces wonderful silk painting projects), and Janet Jones for the Astral star tee-shirt (see page 26).
The manufacturers have been magnificent in their supply of products and advice. Details of their products and contact addresses are in the stockist information section of this book (see previous page), but special thanks go to Dylon, Philip and Tacey, Edding, FW Bramwell Ltd, and Creative Beadcraft.
I would also like to thank the following persons of excellence who all contributed in their own splendid ways. Jane Donovan and Emma Callery for turning endless words and projects into a book; Carole Perks for creating a book it would fit into; Jon and Barbara Stewart for taking the photographs; and all the models for looking great.
The publishers wish to thank Creativity, 45 New Oxford Street, London WC1 (telephone: 0171 240 2945) for supplying materials for photography.